"Karen Ehman's book *A Life That Says Welcome* is full of practical wisdom and ideas that can make your life more enjoyable and your home a more loving place to be. She believes in opening her heart, and her book shows us many ways we can learn to do the same—not only to strangers (fairly easy) but also to family and friends (usually a bit more difficult). The arts of hospitality and of keeping a home are benefits you'll gain from her book. I heartily recommend it."

Jeff Campbell, author of *Speed Cleaning, Clutter Control,* and *Spring Cleaning*

"Wouldn't it be fun to have Martha Stewart, Betty Crocker, and Shirley Dobson as your next-door neighbors? Well, okay, maybe not. How about something even better—your very own "mentor in a book"! Karen Ehman is all of those wonderful influences without the intimidation. If you've ever longed for someone to demonstrate what it means to truly make your house a home, then your (and my) prayers have been answered."

Lisa Whelchel, bestselling author of *Creative Correction,* *The Facts of Life and Other Lessons My Father Taught Me,* and *Taking Care of the "Me" in Mommy*

"From recipes to centerpieces to creative cleaning, Karen shows you how to have 'fun' as a family while learning to care for others."

Susan Alexander Yates, bestselling author of several books including *And Then I Had Teenagers: Encouragement for Parents of Teens and Preteens*

"This book should be read by everyone who wants to sprinkle more joy in their life and home. Though I am no Betty Crocker, I feel inspired to grab my spatula and whip up some homemade hospitality for family and friends alike. Thank you, Karen, for giving us this inspirational book that should be on every woman's bookshelf!"

Lysa TerKeurst, author, speaker, president of
Proverbs 31 Ministries

"Karen's book offers a good background in hospitality and today's form of entertaining as excellent ideas on how to put theory into practice."

Emilie Barnes, author, speaker,
founder of More Hours in My Day

"Karen has provided us with yet another gem! With her usual warm candor, she has opened her life to us, showing all of us how to easily apply hospitality in our everyday lives. Everyone will be better for reading this book."

Jonni McCoy, *Miserly Moms*

"Reading a book by Karen Ehman is like sitting down and sharing a cup of tea with a girlfriend. She's honest, practical, and always has a great sense of humor. If you've struggled to know how to extend hospitality in the midst of raising a family, Karen's practical strategies will help you open your heart and your home to whomever God sends your way!"

Jill Savage, mother of five, executive director of Hearts at Home

"With warmth, wit, practical ideas, and fantastic recipes, Karen has created 'Cliff's Notes' on hospitality that even a busy, stressed-out, non-Martha-Stewart-type woman can enjoy and use in her daily life."

Pam Farrel, international speaker and bestselling author
of *Got Teens?* and *10 Best Decisions a Parent Can Make*

A Life That Says
WELCOME

*Simple Ways to Open Your
Heart & Home to Others*

KAREN EHMAN

Revell
Grand Rapids, Michigan

© 2006 by Karen Ehman

Published by Revell
a division of Baker Publishing Group
P.O. Box 6287, Grand Rapids, MI 49516-6287
www.revellbooks.com

Printed in the United States of America

Library of Congress Cataloging-in-Publication Data
Ehman, Karen, 1964–
    A life that says welcome : simple ways to open your heart & home to others / Karen Ehman.
        p.   cm.
    ISBN 10: 0-8007-3139-5 (pbk.)
    ISBN 978-0-8007-3139-7 (pbk.)
    1. Hospitality—Religious aspects—Christianity. 2. Christian women—Religious life. I. Title.
BV4647.H67E46 2006
241'.671—dc22   2006011130

To my "other mothers"

My spiritual mother, Patricia Esch:
For caring enough to reach out
to a crazy, mixed-up teenager while
lovingly showing her the way to salvation,
I dedicate this book to you.
Your life is a portrait of welcome and comfort.

and to

My mother-in-law, Shirley Ehman:
For "un-birthday" surprises, lovingly cooked meals,
and your ever-gentle reminder that
"we are the sum of our choices,"
I also dedicate this book to you.
How thankful I am that my choice of husband
came with a mother-in-love like you.
Time to celebrate!
(Don't worry, I'll bring the Cool Whip!)

Contents

Acknowledgments 9

1. A Heart That Says "Welcome" 11
2. A Look in the Book 21
3. Family First 41
4. Cleaning and Clutter, Dustballs and Dirt 63
5. The Myth of the Too-Small House 89
6. Decorating on a Shoestring 105
7. Sure, Stay for Supper! 127
8. Here Is the Church, Here Is the Steeple, Open Your Hearts and Bless All the People 153
9. Hospitality on the Road 185
10. Practice Makes Perfect 199
11. God's Bigger Picture 229

Acknowledgments

One seldom writes a book alone, and this one is certainly no exception. There are many to whom I am indebted, for they have served as examples, mentors, and encouragers as I have spoken and written on this topic. I offer them all my heartfelt thanks.

My mother, Margaret Patterson, for serving as the original "hospitality on the road" gal. You have touched so many with your clever gifts, persistent prayers, and comforting company. The only thing better than having you for a mother is knowing my children get you for their grandma!

My wonderful in-laws, the Ehmans. Thank you for your continual examples of hospitality, your patience with me, and your unconditional love. I am proud to bear your last name.

My decades-long mentors: Suzy Williams, Debi Davis, Marcia Stump, and Andie Cocco. So much of what I have learned about being a welcoming wife, mother, and woman of God has come by way of your godly examples and your willingness to tell me of your mistakes and failures in hopes that I can do better. I'm still trying!

Friends Carmen Harmon, Ellen Morse, Jill Kaltenthaler, Karen Leif, Jayne Penfield, and Tammy Underwood. Your support in my writing and speaking ventures and your own keen senses of decorating know-how and culinary expertise are such an encouragement to me!

My sweet (and a few sassy—you know who you are) sisters at Heart at Home Ministries. How I love working with you to bring ideas and refreshment to moms each year at our conferences, in print, and on the Web. Special thanks to the "Michigan gals"—Trisha Hufnagel, Julie Gill, Sherry Nichols, Dorothy Whitcomb, and Pam Snyder—for keeping me humble, stopping often for eighty-nine-cent gas station "cappuccinos," and hauling my books across state lines.

Friends Karen Andrews, Cindy Rose, Roseanne Schafer, Mary Simon, and Marcia Stump. You were the picture of hospitality to a severely sick, pregnant woman with two little ones in tow, allowing her to occupy your couch while you cared for her children for months on end. I will never forget it.

Coauthors and friends Kelly Hovermale and Trish Smith. Writing a book alone is certainly more work! I miss brainstorming with you while sipping herb tea and most of all Trish's fast-typing fingers.

Friends Tim and Audrey Swanson, for unlimited access to your guesthouse, "the summer kitchen," so I could write in peaceful and pleasant surroundings. Talk about hospitality!

Accountability partner Mary Steinke, for words of truth spoken sweetly but seriously, clever cards that arrive just when I need them, and obedience to the Spirit's prompting to intercede for me immediately and then call to ask why. As Kenzie says, "Wow, mom. Freaky!" Observing your life propels me to pray.

My Baker-Revell family. Editors Jeanette Thomason and Lonnie Hull-DuPont; Designer Cheryl VanAndel, and Assistant Managing Editor Kristin Kornoelje. Thank you for believing in me and working so hard to make this book a reality.

My family—husband Todd and children Mackenzie, Mitchell, and Spencer. You are my taste-testers, my cheerleaders, and above all my reason for attempting to show God's love on earth. Mom is all done typing now. Pop the popcorn and get out Uno Attack.

Finally, my Lord and Savior, Jesus Christ. Thank you for offering permanent welcome to me over a quarter of a century ago and assuring me of a future home in heaven. You are the very air I breathe.

∞ 1 ∞

A Heart That Says "Welcome"

The portrait hung in the fireside chapel of our quaint country church. I studied it in detail many a Sunday morning—when I should have been listening to the lesson at hand! It was a famous print of Jesus laughing. Yes, laughing! Our Savior's countenance did not carry a serious, somber look. Instead it sported an all-out, can-hardly-hold-it-in, belly-laughing grin. I simply loved that painting. It comforted me as a young woman to know that even with the grave importance of his mission on earth, occasionally Jesus laughed.

I believe he still does. In fact, I'm sure he is snickering right now as you pick up this book. Why? Well, if you had polled my graduating class of 1982 in the quaint Midwestern town of Grand Ledge, Michigan, and asked them, "Who from our class would be the least likely to ever write a book on hospitality?" I would have won hands down.

It's not that I grew up in a home with a mother who didn't know how to cook. On the contrary, my mother was (and still is) an excellent cook. As a child she first acquired her culinary skills by helping out in the diner her parents owned in southern Indiana. A few years later she worked in a German restaurant, and then, when married, she helped my father in his career as a caterer, coming up with many of the recipes he was well known for. But by the time I reached junior high school, she found herself the single mother of two children. To support our family she took on a career in food service. However, with all the responsibilities of running a home, working full time, and raising two teenagers, she didn't have time to give her own daughter many extensive cooking lessons. When I graduated from high school, my culinary repertoire included boiling water, making instant coffee, and my specialty—an occasional batch of tasty "slice and bake" cookies.

With my mom as the only breadwinner, we were forced to live on a budget so tight it squeaked. We were able to remain living in the home my parents had built ten years earlier, although we weren't able to afford fancy new furnishings to decorate the house. My brother and I busied ourselves with after-school activities, part-time jobs, and homework. None of us was home very much. My mom worked full time, including many late evenings. All of this added up to the fact that we didn't often invite others into our home. During all my school-age years, I never had a slumber party, had a friend spend the night, or even had a girlfriend ride the bus home with me after school to visit for a few hours. I have no recollection of anyone ever coming to our house for dinner, and the only overnight guests we ever entertained were the relatives who came once a year from Milwaukee.

I knew my mother felt terrible about all of this as her "white picket fence" dreams gave way to the harsh reality of life as a single parent. And I felt bad too. I remember so desperately wanting to learn to cook and decorate and have others over. I would sometimes cut out pictures of beautiful homes from the pages of decorating magazines and secretly stash them in a folder for future reference when I had a home of my own someday.

Realizing that my mom was doing her best to keep the home running, hot food on the table, and some degree of normalcy in our home, I decided I would do something nice for her. So I turned where I often have in my life—to books. I specifically remember one day in early high school getting out the 1960 edition of the big, red Betty Crocker cookbook with Betty's portrait on the cover. (You *do* realize that she isn't an actual person, don't you? She is just an artist's conceptual drawing whose hairdo they update every few years. Just checking!) That afternoon Betty and I were going to make a banana cream pie to surprise my mom when she returned home from a hard day's work.

Now, I was intelligent enough. I was getting *almost* straight A's in my ninth-grade year of high school, knowing I had to win a scholarship if I wanted to go to college. But the only class I wasn't pulling an A in was (you guessed it) home ec. Our teacher decided we would make what I call an "anybody can sew pattern"—the kind that's supposed to be extremely easy and take no more than two hours. The project took me the better part of three weeks, and I still wasn't finished. As a result, that was the only class I ever received a B in, and it kept me from graduating as class valedictorian. (Mrs. Christman, I forgive you.)

As I sat at the dining room table that rainy Saturday afternoon, staring at Betty's mug on the front of my mom's cookbook, I knew this was different. This wasn't sewing. It was baking, and I could handle it. All I needed to do was to follow the full-color, step-by-step instructions for a banana cream pie.

Follow them I did, to a T. Only Miss Crocker had neglected to tell me how ripe the bananas should be. I was sure I remembered my mother mentioning something about the bananas needing to be really black and mushy in order to make a great banana cream pie. Or was that banana *bread*? Well, I thought it was pie. So I peeled and sliced three of the blackest Chiquitas I could find and then meticulously followed Miss Crocker's directions.

Can you envision what this creation looked like when I was through?

Still, I left it out on the table for my mom to see when she arrived home after her shift at work. Taking a seat in the living room, I awaited her squeal of thankful delight as she saw my labor of love, a heartfelt gesture done out of honest appreciation. I beamed at the thought.

Had my mother known the emotional damage she would cause me to this day by her reaction, I'm sure she would have responded differently. For instead of sweetly encouraging my homemaking efforts, she burst out in laughter and ran to the hall closet, snatching up the Polaroid camera to take a picture to preserve for all eternity. I've often told her that one of these days she'll be sorry when she turns on the television and hears, *"Homemakers who were laughed at as children and the mothers who ruined them . . . coming up next on Oprah."*

Now, my little pie fiasco took place during my freshman year, so for the remainder of my four years of high school, I hit the books hard. I followed the easy college prep course of study and stayed away from those killer home ec courses. (In my opinion, schools should rethink the figuring of grade point averages. A student who can pull a four point in cooking, sewing, and early childhood education beats one who breezes through chemistry, trigonometry, and honors English hands down!) At the end of my four years, I had won enough scholarships to attend a Christian college. Once there, I pursued my goal of obtaining a dual degree. I wanted to get my B.A. in social science with a minor in speech. But more importantly (and the real reason I was there),

A Life That Says Welcome

I wanted to secure my MRS. degree, which I promptly did three weeks after graduation.

At that point in my life I saw further proof that God has a sense of humor. You see, the man I met and fell in love with was probably the worst one on campus to marry a domestically challenged gal, for here is the female makeup of his family:

- His mother, like mine, is a fabulous cook. She sewed costumes for each of her five children when they were growing up and hand knit them sweaters, socks, and beautifully intricate Christmas stockings. She has a home tastefully decorated with antiques, and she regularly offers heartfelt hospitality to others.

- He has three sisters. The first one lives in a charming 150-year-old farmhouse just outside of Washington, DC. The second sister lives in a stunning home in the wooded countryside and offers catering to area businesses in addition to working in the interior decorating field. The third sister founded a bed-and-breakfast near West Palm Beach, Florida, which she and her husband completely restored. Oh, and she's a marketing, decorating, and culinary dynamo.

Imagine the scene as I proudly showed up to my first Ehman Thanksgiving with my "bake and take" Sara Lee pie from the frozen foods section. In the early days I relied a lot on my two best friends—Sara Lee and Mrs. Smith—and I always volunteered to bring the pie. Thinking myself quite clever, I also brought a container of Cool Whip.

I now know this is a mortal sin in Ehman eyes. The Ehmans don't use Cool Whip. They've never used Cool Whip. They would *never* use Cool Whip. They buy fresh cream from the creamery and whip it themselves.

Thankfully, they are gracious, loving, forgiving people and were very long-suffering with me when I married into their family twenty years ago and took on their last name, which could have been the demise of all their hard-earned reputations.

But I hate to admit to you that I did not want to be outdone by these ladies. I wanted to show them that I could be artsy-smartsy too.

Again, I turned to books. I trekked off to the library in our little town of Three Rivers, Michigan. I checked out every book that had the word "entertaining" in the title. I read *The Joy of Cooking* from cover to cover. But I stayed away from Betty Crocker because I had already been burned by Betty once. I learned to make fancy *hors d'oeuvres* and to bake a double-crust pie from scratch, and I even once, but only once, sewed my own kitchen valances.

I was determined that our tiny apartment would look like one of the homes featured in the pages of *Country Living* magazine—perfectly decorated with exquisite furniture and coordinating decorator fabrics. There would be loaves of homemade whole wheat bread nestled in antique baskets alongside sparkling jars of jams and jellies and beautiful berry pies cooling on the counter. There was only one problem. We were living on my husband's youth pastor salary and obviously weren't in the same income bracket as the dear folks featured in the pages of *Country Living* magazine. And I noticed something about those pages: there were never any people in those pictures, let alone children. What would we do when they came along? Hide the diapers and baby wipes in an antique cedar trunk? Hang a lovely potted fern in the baby swing and hope no one would notice?

At the same time all of this was going on, I was still meeting almost weekly with the pastor's wife from the church I went to while I was in high school. She had first reached out to me when I was a lonely teenager, telling me of a God who could be the Father to the fatherless. As she opened her life to me, the lessons my mother had taught me and the biblical truths she'd tried to instill into me all began to make sense. My mother's prayers were answered as I solidified my decision for Christ and became a believer. Now that I was a young bride, Pat stuck by her commitment to disciple me.

I noticed something about my frequent visits to her home. I always felt that she was thrilled to have me over. She'd have waiting my favorite cup of herbal tea and a throw blanket for me to cuddle up in. She'd fix me lunch and visit with me, asking me about our new marriage. She'd inquire if there was anything at all she could pray about for me. And two things were consistent each time I went to her home.

First, she always had her tattered, worn, brown leather Bible lying open on the counter like she had probably just finished reading it. And second, she didn't just ask me how she could pray for me. She'd stop right then and pray with me in her driveway before I got back into my little Volkswagen Rabbit to make the two-hour trip back home. More than anyplace else on earth, her home made me feel welcomed and pampered while I was there and refreshed when I left.

Now let me tell you about her home: It was an old church parsonage. It hadn't been redecorated in years! Her colors were an array of avocado green, harvest gold, and *Brady Bunch* burnt orange. (What *were* they thinking in the 1970s?) She had shag carpet, which frankly has always given me the creeps because I wonder just what is hiding in there. Many of the items in her home were in desperate need of updating or replacement, but because it was a church parsonage, they couldn't make any changes without first running it by several committees. So they decided they'd just make do. Pat kept her home as charming and clean as she could and regularly opened it up as a haven to whomever God brought her way.

Her lunches were very simple. Sometimes she'd feed me creamed chipped beef served over day-old bread that had been made into toast. She'd chuckle and halfway apologize because that was what her father had eaten in the army. But you know what? It tasted like a gourmet feast when I was in her presence.

And all of those books I had been poring over trying to be the perfect hostess? Well, it was through this dear mentor, my friend Pat, that I finally wised up and realized I had been reading the wrong books. They weren't the ones she had lying open on her counter. God began to teach me that there is a huge difference between "entertaining" and offering hospitality. Entertaining puts the emphasis on you and how you can impress others. Offering hospitality puts the emphasis on others and strives to meet their physical and spiritual needs so that they feel refreshed, not impressed, when they leave your home.

Now, it isn't wrong to want to serve good food or have an attractive, clean house. Actually the Bible says to undertake any task at hand as though we were working for God himself (see Col. 3:23). But like so much of life, it all comes down to the motives of your heart. Are you trying to impress others with your entertaining prowess, like I was? Or are you trying to refresh them and point them toward the Lord? I thought entertaining meant you fluffed the cushions each time a guest stood up from the couch and ran around straightening any little thing that got out of place. You know, keep up that perfect "magazine look." Or that I had to plan and execute a five-course meal that had to be baked in a 400-degree oven on a 95-degree July day in an un-air-conditioned apartment the size of a postage stamp, just to impress two of my sisters-in-law with lunch while they were in town. I had to learn the hard way that offering hospitality is much more about the condition of your heart than the condition of your home.

And I've come to realize too that hospitality does not always need to involve your home. Maybe you are someone with limited living space or a woman whose husband does not share your desire to open up your home to others. If that is the case with you, then you are going to need to learn to implement some ideas that I call "hospitality on the road." I think this kind of love in action can be so powerful that I've devoted an entire chapter to it.

So, HGTV wannabes, cooking class dropouts, and hesitant housekeepers, will you join me in the journey to see your life as a channel for God's unconditional love to others within your sphere of influence? Will you shelve your decorating magazines for a while and commit to learning his ways of reaching out to others? Will you dust off your Bible and give your heart a good spring cleaning before you start to scrub your home? If the answer is yes, then listen. Hear God's heartbeat for the lonely, the lost, the less-than-lovely. Determine to be his hands and feet to family and friends alike. Adopt a lifestyle of reaching out to those whom God puts in your path. You won't regret it. I promise.

Points to Ponder

- Can you think of any people in your life who regularly show heartfelt hospitality to others? How have you felt when you were a guest in their home? What specifically did they do that made you feel welcomed?

- Have you made any past attempts at entertaining out of a desire to impress others? What happened? How would you go back and do it differently if you could?

- Think of two or three friends whom you would feel comfortable inviting over. Make arrangements to have just one of them over for a simple lunch in the next two weeks. Remind yourself: hospitality starts somewhere—with small steps!

- What has been your experience when it comes to entertaining? Discuss with a friend what kind of home you came from. Did you have others over often or not? Were you ever a guest, and what good experiences do you remember? How have such experiences influenced your hospitality habits today?

A Look in the Book

ew Look up 1 Peter 4:8–10. What does this passage say about *how* we are to offer hospitality? Does it sound like it is an option or a command? What part does love play? In what ways do you feel this Scripture passage nudging you?

ew How would you rate yourself on the "grumbling and complaining" scale when it comes to offering hospitality? Do you pass with flying colors or flunk out?

ew Read 2 Corinthians 1:3–4. How has God comforted you in the past? How could you in turn use that comfort to reach out to another person going through the same kind of trial? What is a tangible way you could meet their needs, both physically and spiritually?

Putting It into Practice

ew Name someone in your life whom God is nudging you to reach out to. What could you do to help lighten their load? What has been keeping you from contacting them? Time, resources, busyness? How will you go about changing this?

ew How can you carve out time regularly to meet the needs of others? What would have to go? Time spent watching television, sleeping late, shopping, or pursuing hobbies?

ew How can a friend help keep you accountable to change this?

∞ 2 ∞

A Look in the Book

The history of entertaining in America makes for an interesting study. As recent as the 1950s, couples had dinner parties where the mother planned several courses of fancy, impressive foods that were time-consuming to prepare. The children were shuffled off to bed by about 7:00 p.m. and it was an adults-only affair. A different home hosted the party each week. The hostess tried to outdo the gal who had held the party the week before. Shame on you if her crab puffs were flakier than yours! To add to the mix, the need to reciprocate hung thick in the air. Just who was having whom over for dinner was the talk of the town.

Yes, entertaining was a huge American pastime; however, experts were few. Okay, maybe Emily Post was majoring in manners and Betty Crocker could help with those crab cakes, but the climate of "experts for everything" that we witness today did not exist.

Oh yes, today we are surrounded by experts—in books and magazines and on our television screens. In fact, I feel that the reason most women today don't regularly jump at the chance to offer hospitality can be summed up in four letters: HGTV!

We have become obsessed with shows and hosts that show us just how it should be done—the décor, the *hors d'oeuvres*, the entrees, the garden, and more. And what about all of those magazines that stare at you from the doctor's office table? Even their titles can be intimidating: *House Beautiful. Better Homes and Gardens*. (What about us who reside in House Normal or have an Average Home and Garden?) Tragically, we have let the scores of experts scare the aprons off of us. Subconsciously, we feel that if we can't do it like the experts do, then by golly, we won't do it at all!

Now, before you toss all of your magazines and cancel your cable subscription, let me say that I do incorporate some of the experts' ideas into my own hospitality. You know, the not-too-complicated ones where you don't have to actually fly to Sri Lanka to peel the cinnamon bark off of a native evergreen tree to make your pumpkin cheesecake. You can just go to Wal-Mart. But I have had to learn to use the experts and their ideas as resources, not as a lifestyle. There is a balance between occasionally finding a decorating idea or a new recipe to use and letting all of those shows make us discontent.

A few of my friends have confided in me that they have had to actually stop receiving certain catalogs and magazines in the mail. They felt that just poring over their pages made them lose contentment—fast. Am I advising that you give them up too? Not necessarily. You know what you can handle. If you can't glance through a publication or tune in to a TV show without the monster of discontentment rearing its ugly head, then by all means put down the remote or toss the magazine! But if you can use them as a resource to locate some great decorating ideas or yummy recipes without turning sage green with envy, then go right ahead and enjoy.

But should we be taking our cues from the world of décor and gourmet food experts? I've already shared what happened when I tried just such a game plan. Disaster. And what about my mentor Pat and her brown leather Bible? Isn't that the book through which she learned to be so welcoming to me? What guidance does it have to give us?

The word *hospitality*—in the original Greek language *philoxenia*—occurs several times in the New Testament, so it must be significant to God. But what exactly does it mean?

First of all, it means, in its purest form, the love of strangers. There were many opportunities to practice "stranger love" back then. Not a lot of Holy Land Holiday Inns dotted the first-century Palestine map. So many times ordinary families took in strangers who were passing through.

Now before you envision the father of the family bringing a roadside hitchhiker home for dinner on the back of his late-model camel, let me explain. Although at times overnight guests were complete strangers, more often than not they were the friend of a friend or a very distant relative. Suppose you were from the southern city of Beersheba on your way up north to the town of Jericho, which was a distance of about sixty miles. To travel that far meant a journey of several days. In between were several small towns as well as the city of Jerusalem. Perhaps you planned to stay at the inn when your clan reached Jerusalem, but what about the rest of the trip?

Well, at any of the other towns in between, you might have a very distant relative or perhaps a friend of a friend. When you stopped at the town, you'd immediately locate a phone booth and look up their number to let them know to throw the steaks on the grill, you were coming for supper.

Well, kind of. More likely you would inquire at the town square as to the whereabouts of the family you were looking for. Either you would be pointed in the right direction or a messenger would run out to their place to let them know company was coming.

So if you lived during this time, even though you may have heard of the people who were about to lodge at your home, you really didn't know them. They were in many respects strangers. You may have heard about Great-Uncle Hezekiah's hearty laugh or Aunt Lydia's long beautiful hair, but since no one could shoot you a heads-up email with a digital picture of them attached, you had no idea what they looked like.

In New Testament times you simply had to be ready year-round for just such unexpected company. Funny how today we can have several days' or even weeks' notice that company is coming, but we stress about just such scenarios. New Testament Christians simply welcomed these people, inviting them to join in for a few days as they went about their daily routine. Maybe we should take a cue from them.

A Welcome Heart

I am convinced that hospitality means more than just taking in an occasional visitor overnight. Take a quick trip through the New Testament verses on hospitality and you'll notice something right away. It is nearly impossible to separate the word *hospitality* from another New Testament word. That word is *phileo*, one of the words rendered "love" in the Bible. Its meaning denotes tender affection from one person to another; brotherly or sisterly love; the kind of love that says, "No, after you. . . ." We can seek to practice this kind of love on a day-to-day basis on our way to becoming a person whose very life says "welcome."

Have you ever known that kind of person? Someone warm, inviting, comforting; someone who makes you feel secure and at home no matter where you are; someone who, when you are a little down in the dumps, helps you begin to climb out just by seeing her face? She makes you feel a little more at ease no matter where you may happen to have your feet planted at the minute. What is different about her? She is hospitable throughout her life, not just within her four walls. She not only opens her home but opens her heart as well.

These are the people who take their hospitality on the road. They have a ministry of welcoming, comforting, and encouraging others wherever they may be. Later on we will be discussing several tangible ideas for offering hospitality on the road. For now, we'll focus on what type of person we should be in order to do so.

So back to the Bible. What other insight does God's Word give us in our quest to be a hospitable person? Flip through its pages and you'll see just how else the word *hospitality* was used.

God thinks so much of this character quality that he lists it as a requirement for anyone desiring to be a deacon or overseer in the church (see 1 Tim. 3:2 and Titus 1:8). Now lest you think that lets the rest of us off scot-free, keep flipping. In 1 Peter 4:9 *all* Christians are told to offer hospitality without . . . can anyone finish it?

Without grumbling. You know: hands on hips, eyes rolled, mouth wide open complaining and griping, citing every excuse in the book for why this is just *not* a good idea. "Well, I would have others over to our house, it's just that our house is way too small!" or "We can't have that new family at church over. You've seen their children—they're totally unruly! They'll never take their shoes off on this new light-colored carpet. Uh-uh . . . not them. No way."

Confession time. Both of those phrases rolled flippantly off the lips of yours truly in my not-so-distant past. However, this verse implies that grumble-free hospitality is not an optional activity. No matter the translation, you won't find the words, "Now, *if* you decide you'd like to offer hospitality to someone, then for Pete's sake, be nice." Oh, wouldn't that let us off of the hospitality hook!

Sorry. We're all hooked with this one. This sentence in Scripture is written more as a command: "Offer hospitality . . . without grumbling" (1 Peter 4:9). The writer's assumption is that we will do it and we'll have the right attitude when we do. So we'd better decide now to chuck our excuses and start obeying God's command to use our homes and our lives as an avenue for his love to others.

Did you know that the Bible even goes so far as to say that by offering hospitality to strangers, some have unknowingly entertained angels (see Heb. 13:2)? Wouldn't that be exciting? When they were small, our children loved for us to invite strangers home from church. They were hoping to get a glimpse of an angel!

The Infamous Examples

If you've ever heard a sermon on or read an article in a Christian magazine about hospitality, no doubt those infamous sisters Mary and Martha were used as an example. We catch their story in Luke 10:38–42.

> As Jesus and his disciples were on their way, he came to a village where a woman named Martha opened her home to him. She had a sister called Mary, who sat at the Lord's feet listening to what he said. But Martha was distracted by all the preparations that had to be made. She came to him and asked, "Lord, don't you care that my sister has left me to do the work by myself? Tell her to help me!"
>
> "Martha, Martha," the Lord answered, "you are worried and upset about many things, but only one thing is needed. Mary has chosen what is better, and it will not be taken away from her."

If you've encountered commentary on these siblings before, the spin put on it was probably that Mary was right and Martha was in the wrong. You know—good sister, bad sister. But it is interesting that Jesus did not say that what Martha was doing was wrong. Look again. He said that she was upset and worried about the many preparations that had to be made. I mean, when someone is coming to dine at your house, especially a big someone like Jesus was, with crowds of people following him around and all, well, you just naturally have a little work to do before the party starts. Planning and preparing have their rightful place in offering hospitality. So what was Martha's big problem?

One we still battle today: She was distracted, sidetracked, preoccupied. Her attention was diverted from the important and riveted on the trivial. Simply stated, her priorities were all out of whack!

Her sister, however, was not so. In fact, instead of a chewing out, Mary gets an "atta girl" from the Lord right out there in public. What does it say Jesus saw in Mary that was absent in Martha? She had chosen "what is better" that would not be taken away from her. The Amplified Bible even reads this way: "Mary has chosen the good portion (that which is to her advantage)" (v. 42). What could possibly be to her advantage that would not be able to be taken away?

Her relationship with the Lord.

You see, Mary wasn't running to and fro, fretting and fussing. She was picking a better plan. She was intently listening to the Lord's words, realizing that his words embedded in her heart were good and could never be taken away. The fish sticks and fig pie (or whatever was on the menu that day) would not last. But the Word of the Lord would stand forever (see Isa. 40:8).

This account tells us not only what Mary was doing but also where she was doing it. She was listening to the Lord's words while seated at his feet. Being seated at his feet denotes a humble act of service. Feet in those days were pretty filthy from walking in sandals along the dusty roads of Jerusalem, but that was where she was best able to hear the Lord's word to her. And I feel that today when we take on a humble role, serving the less than lovely or serving when we have to get dirty (or our carpet has to get dirty!), well, it is then that we are best positioned to hear the Lord's word to us, just as Mary was.

Which Sister Are You?

Now I think most women tend either to be more of a Mary, whose strength was a life of devotion, or a Martha, whose strength was a life of service. I see this illustrated three or four times a year as I take part in a nondenominational ministry to moms known as Hearts at Home.

Each year we put on conferences designed to educate, equip, and encourage moms in their jobs at home serving their families. At conference time we get ready to practice hospitality and practice it *big*. Our spring national conference alone draws in more than six thousand women for a weekend of keynote speakers, musical guests, dramas, and workshops tailor-made to fit their various stages of mothering. Above all we desire that these precious moms feel welcome, wanted, and pampered. But how?

We provide them with a nice tote bag full of useful materials and always plenty of chocolate. We place smiles on our faces and friendly attitudes in our hearts, ready to answer their questions and to help solve any problems or glitches in their schedule. We have the surroundings, including the main stage and luncheon tables, tastefully decorated. Shoot, we even go crazy with the bathrooms. Baskets of lotions, hairspray, safety pins, and other essentials on the counters; attractive signs on the insides of the stall doors sporting encouraging quotes on motherhood. We even transform the men's bathrooms into lovely ladies' rooms

A Life That Says Welcome

complete with beautiful green potted ferns carefully placed in the scrubbed-down urinals. (We affectionately refer to these make-shift planters as "fernals"!)

On conference setup day the place is abuzz. It has been interesting for me to watch these dear sisters of mine throughout the years that we have been offering these conferences. There is a lot of "Martha" work to be done—setting up registration tables and readying the main stage, the book and resource tables, those pretty bathrooms, and on and on and on. However, we have made it a priority, under the leadership of our founder and director Jill Savage, to be first of all people of prayer. We begin months ahead with prayer both in groups and as individuals. On setup day, we stop at midday for praise and worship and to pray corporately before splitting off on our own prayer walks to ask God to work in the hearts of the women who will attend.

It has helped us to maintain our balance by focusing more on God and his Word than the setup required when expecting thousands of guests. If we didn't, who knows what disaster might befall us on setup day? I imagine it would be an all-out Mary-Martha war. The Marthas would be frantically scrambling about trying to get set up, all the while yelling at the Marys to get off their knees and do something constructive, for crying out loud! Sadly, I admit to you that I'm afraid I would be at the head of the Martha pack, leading the charge! Because Hearts at Home has been an organization committed to prayer, this has not happened. When it had its beginnings in the early nineties, before we ever held our first conference, an entire year was devoted to praying and seeking God, just as Mary did, before attempting any Martha-style work.

But please, let's not give Miss Martha a bum rap. In other places in Scripture we can see her serving and serving mightily (see John 11:19–37; 12:1–2). She was very special to Jesus and crucial to his earthly ministry. Perhaps the lesson we can learn from this story is that the Marthas among us need to work more on preparing our hearts to serve others before we prepare our homes—but maybe some of you Marys need to learn to help us with the housework!

You see, any strength carried to an extreme can become a weakness. (If you let that phrase soak in a minute, I'll bet you can think of a dozen examples!) But do you know who was a perfect blend of Mary and Martha's good qualities? Jesus was. You will notice if you read through the New Testament that when our Lord encountered someone, he usually met the physical need of that person first. If they were hungry, he fed them. If they were sick, he healed them. Then he focused on their heart and its condition.

Practice Makes Perfect

Let's look at another use of the word *hospitality* in the New Testament. In Romans 12:13 God's Word says to "practice hospitality." Webster's dictionary defines *practice* this way: "To do or perform habitually; to make a habit of; to exercise or perform repeatedly in order to acquire or polish a skill."

When I hear the word *practice*, I think of my daughter trying years ago to learn to play the violin. Out of her bedroom arose sounds of screeching and scratching and then, eventually, the familiar notes of *The Sound of Music* emanating from that fiddle. Or I think of my son, who has his Hit-a-Way batting practice baseball on a cord attached to the basketball hoop in our front yard. As I stand at my kitchen sink doing the dishes, I can hear the loud, metal-sounding *plink, plink, plink* from the repetitive pounding of that ball as he gets ready to play for our local team. What do each of these childhood examples have in common? Both began at a place of no knowledge or skill. But with a stick-to-it attitude and opportunity to implement what they learned, both became able to perform what they were attempting to do.

It is the same with hospitality. Maybe you feel you lack skill or motivation or both. But God's Word cheers us on, "Just practice!" So practice we must. Whether you live in an apartment, a modest home, or a mansion, you are not exempt from our Father's admonition that you show hospitality to his children and those who are yet to be his children. Yes, our being willing to offer hospitality can help lead people to new life in Christ.

In college I had the honor of meeting the late Francis Schaeffer and his lovely wife Edith. The Schaeffers began as a couple who regularly opened their home to whomever God brought their way. In the end, they were well known for their writing and speaking but mostly for their ministry L'Abri Fellowship. L'Abri was a place where sojourners from all walks of life were welcomed, fed, and pampered but most importantly challenged by Dr. Schaeffer's well-thought-out arguments for the validity of Christianity. Their little ministry didn't stay little for long as scores of converts emerged from within their four walls and spread out to the four corners of the earth.

What amazes me most is how these lives were touched through the simple but kind gestures of Mrs. Schaeffer's hands and heart. She welcomed them and made their rooms and beds inviting. She cooked and cleaned again and again in order to show them the love of Christ. These people, skeptics and believers alike, lived day in and day out with Francis and Edith and their children. They were given an up close and personal glimpse of the kingdom through the life of a normal family. This healthy dose of Christian hospitality whetted their appetites for the things of the Lord. The minds of these soon-to-be believers were able to respond to Dr. Schaeffer's challenges because their souls were already filled with Mrs. Schaeffer's love. Perhaps as many lives were changed for eternity through Mrs. Schaeffer's simple homemaking as through Dr. Schaeffer's excellent teaching.

It can be the same for you, dear reader. Perhaps not in the same magnitude, but in exactly the way God has planned for your family. Your family has been placed on this earth at this exact point and time. It is not an accident. Who does God want to bless through your willingness to open your home?

Being There . . . *Really* There

I read a quote once by the late missionary Jim Elliot that said simply this: "Wherever you are, be all there."

Boy, is that hard for a multitasking momma like me! Wherever I am, I am thinking of four other places where I will be needed or seven other things I could be doing to get myself finally caught up. I am not even half there most of the time. I'm one-quarter there, at best. But oh, what a worthy goal! Wherever you are, be all there.

I know some little people who can tell instantly when you're not. Have you ever noticed how observant and perceptive children can be? They can almost always tell when you are really listening and when you are simply staring like the proverbial deer in the headlights while your mind is totally elsewhere. They certainly can tell if you are being "all there."

Take my eight-year-old, Spencer. Ever since he was old enough to participate, he has loved to play board games. On the other hand, when I play board games I get, well, bored. But I have noticed how easily it can shrink his spirit when I play a game of Monopoly with him while making out my shopping list, catch a round of Trouble while polishing my toenails, or attempt to take part in a family Uno Attack tournament while talking on the phone. My dear ones, this should not be! Wherever we are, we need to be all there. It is the first step toward developing a welcoming heart and hospitable demeanor.

My friend Betsy Salisbury is just the opposite of me. The eighth child of ten, she grew up with a mother who welcomed not only her own children but all the ones in the neighborhood as well. It was said of her mom that she raised her own ten children as well as a couple dozen or so more who took up regular residence in their backyard sandbox. Like her mom, Betsy is a magnet for children, especially my boys. Betsy, as a rule, knows how to be "all there."

When preparing to give my first talk on hospitality six years ago, I decided to enlist the help of my children. Since they are where I get some comic relief and also my best material, I decided to interview them each on the topic at hand.

First I explained to them just what it means to be hospitable. Then I asked them if they could name anybody they knew whom they felt was such a person. Then-five-year-old Mitchell was the first to pipe up.

"Hey . . . I know who is 'spitable," he chimed. I smiled as I asked him who he was thinking of.

He continued, "Mrs. Salisbury is." When I questioned why he chose Betsy, this was his reply: "You can tell she loves little boys, Mom. She takes us down to the fishin' hole. And she lets us jump on her furniture, eat homemade peanut butter cookies straight out of the oven, and paint her garden rocks with purple nail polish." All apparently vital components of hospitality according to a five-year-old boy!

My children are not the only ones who are drawn to Betsy and her home. Two of her neighbor girls became a real part of the Salisbury family on an ongoing basis while their parents went through a difficult and sad divorce. As the girls began to be shuffled from parent to parent, Betsy's home became a constant and a safe haven for these girls. Her family naturally blended these two precious souls into their daily existence. They went with the family to Vacation Bible School and the AWANA scouting program at church. They shared snacks and movies, meals and overnights. They ran through the sprinkler and watched Mr. Salisbury's crazy juggling routine.

They became a part of the family. These girls felt they belonged. In fact, one day when the Salisburys got their family portrait back from the photographer, one of the neighbor girls, upon hearing it referred to as a family picture, glanced over it and asked, "Well then, where are we?"

Through the love and acceptance the Salisburys had shown, these two precious ones had come to feel that they weren't just neighbors, they were a part of the family. Is there anyone who feels they should be part of your family portrait?

As you work your way through the chapters of this book, my prayer for you is this: that you too will begin to see your current lot in life—the home you now live in, the neighborhood in which that home sits, the church you now attend, even the grocery store you shop at—as a divine appointment. I pray that you will trust God and remember that what he calls us to do, he enables us to do. Don't waste your life playing the "if only" game—"If only I had a bigger house, finer china, nicer furniture, a kinder, more gentle husband . . . why, then I'd go for this hospitality thing." STOP. Determine to use whatever resources you may now have for God's glory. It will be an adventure through which you will not only give blessing but also receive it in return.

So no more excuses. Roll up your sleeves. It's time to practice.

A Life That Says Welcome

☜Welcome Ideas☞

Inspirational Examples

When looking for examples of those who lived a life of hospitality and kindheartedness, we need only to open a Bible and read. Those oft-cited sisters Mary and Martha aren't the only ones from whom we can learn. The pages of Scripture present profiles of both men and women who serve as inspiration by leaving behind a legacy of love.

Sarah and Abraham (Genesis 18:1–15)—This famous couple was given a unique opportunity to offer hospitality. The account begins in their temporary home in the oak grove at Mamre. One day near noon, Abraham was quietly sitting at the entrance to his tent. All at once he noticed three strangers standing nearby. Scripture says he got up and ran to meet them, bowing low to the ground, a traditional posture of welcome. He urged them to stop and rest and offered them the cool shade of his trees, fresh water to wash their feet, and something to eat. When they agreed to stay, he ran to tell the missus that company was here and yes, they'd be staying for supper. Sarah whipped up some hot loaves of bread while Abraham worked on roasting some meat and gathering some cheese curds and milk to round out the meal. Their hearts were willing and their hands were able to welcome these three into their home. Through these three strangers the Lord revealed his plan to give them a son by that same time next year.

Boaz (Ruth 2:1–4:12)—In his kindhearted and clever way, this man offered hospitality to a young woman and received her as his wife in return! It began with his simple offer of bread and grain and a place to sleep at night. Through his obedience Boaz and his new bride were included in the ancestry of Jesus—they are listed in the genealogy found in the Gospel of Matthew.

Abigail (1 Samuel 25:1–42)—She seemed to have it all. She was gorgeous and intelligent and had a heart for hospitality. She was even married to an immensely rich man. There was one slight problem. Her husband, Nabal, was rude, dishonest, and terribly ill-mannered. At this time, soon-to-be-king David and his band of close companions were hiding from Saul, who was seeking David's life after finding that the prophet Samuel had already anointed David as king. It was sheep shearing time, and David and crew had been providing protection for Nabal's flocks out in the countryside. Thinking Nabal surely was pleased, David sent word to him asking for any provisions he could spare for the group of men. Instead, Nabal reacted by calling them a wandering band of outlaws. When Abigail heard of her husband's insulting behavior, she went to find David, who was on his way with four hundred men with swords. She quickly gathered a huge assortment of bread, wine, sheep, grain, and, for dessert, raisin and fig cakes and sent them ahead of her on donkeys. Talk about meals on wheels, uh, er . . . hooves! She met David, bowed low, and apologized for her husband's bad behavior, going so far as to take all of the blame on herself. She spoke truth to David as she recounted his kindness and asserted that he was fighting the Lord's battles. He accepted her gifts and her polite words and let her husband live. God later killed Nabal, and David wound up taking the sweet and clever Abigail as his own wife.

Rahab (Joshua 2:1–21; 6:17–25)—This woman was said to practice a shady career, but she serves as an inspiring and courageous example to us today. She willingly and at great risk hid the two spies who were sent by Joshua to size up the land of Jericho and its inhabitants. When men came to search out the spies, she cunningly sent their pursuers on a wild goose chase. Later, when the city of Jericho fell and its inhabitants were killed, Rahab and her family had their lives spared. They were rescued as promised by being located by a scarlet cord strung down from their window. If God can use a harlot and her ready and willing heart, he can use any one of us!

The Widow of Zarephath (1 Kings 17:8–24)—God told the prophet Elijah to stop by the village of Zarephath and have supper at the home of a poor widow there. When he arrived and found her, he asked for water to drink and some bread to eat. With the water she was willing, but when it came to baking bread, she lamented, "I don't have any bread—only a handful of flour in a jar and a little oil in a jug. I am gathering a few sticks to take home and make a meal for myself and my son, that we may eat it—and die" (1 Kings 17:12). But God had not planned that ending to her life. Elijah gave her instructions to make some bread for him first and then to feed herself and her son without any worry. There would always be oil and flour left in her jars to make more bread until the Lord sent rain and the crops began to grow again. She did as he said, and her cupboard was never bare during the long drought that followed. Simple food, a willing heart. You can have both, can't you?

The Shunammite woman (2 Kings 4:8–37)—A well-to-do woman lived in the Old Testament town of Shunem. When the prophet Elisha happened by her place, she offered him comfort and some food to eat. From then on, he became a regular at this makeshift restaurant as he found her doors always open and food on the table. The eager hostess and her husband even made a guest room up on the roof, complete with a bed, a table, a chair, and a lamp, so that Elisha would have a place to lodge each time he came to their town. The Lord repaid this kind gesture by giving this couple the one thing they most wanted—a baby boy!

Priscilla and Aquila (Acts 18:1–28; Romans 16:3; 1 Corinthians 16:19; 2 Timothy 4:19)—This husband-wife team took in the apostle Paul in the town of Corinth. They lived and worked side by side, earning their wages as tentmakers. This business partnership became the foundation for a lasting friendship between the three. They later accompanied Paul to the coast of Syria. Later, Paul departed Ephesus, but they remained behind. They encountered a man named Apollos, an eloquent speaker who knew the Scriptures well but only taught of John's baptism. Priscilla and Aquila took him aside and gently explained the way of God to him more accurately. With their love and instruction, he went on to be a powerful preacher, accurately handling the Word of God and boldly refuting the Jews in public debate. Other places in the New Testament we find warm greetings flowing both to and from this devoted couple. We are told a church met regularly in their home. Paul said that they had risked their lives for him and that all of the Gentile churches were so thankful for this remarkable couple. Why were they remarkable? They simply obeyed God by living a life of welcome both at home and on the road.

Lydia (Acts 16:11–15)—Lydia was a seller of purple cloth from the city of Thyatira. She had an open heart and willing spirit that resulted in the baptism of her entire household after she heard Paul speak about Christ. Immediately she opened her house for Paul and his friends to stay for a while.

Dorcas (Acts 9:36–42)—This woman of Joppa, also called Tabitha, was well known for her good deeds and active love for the poor. She also was skilled in making wonderful cloaks and other garments. One day she became ill and died. Her friends began to mourn and prepare her body for burial. Soon her friends asked Peter to come. He witnessed the outpouring of their love. The Lord was so touched by her deeds and the devotion of her sorrowful friends that through Peter, he raised Dorcas from the dead. Apparently he felt she still had more sewing and serving to do! Perhaps your work for the Lord is at a standstill. He still works today. He can resurrect your lapsed desire to scatter kindness on his behalf.

Other unsung, sometimes unnamed New Testament characters—Remember the nameless lad who gave Jesus five loaves of bread and two fish (John 6:1–14)? Through his willing generosity over five thousand hungry people were fed. What about the women of Galilee who were said to follow Jesus, caring for his needs (Matthew 27:54–56)? Mary Magdalene, Jesus's mother Mary, and the mother of disciples James and John are the only three specifically mentioned, but it says more took part. They were willing to travel and look out for the needs of our Lord while receiving no recognition in return. What about the unnamed islanders of Malta who willingly welcomed the shipwrecked Paul and his entire entourage (Acts 28:1–10)? Scripture states that they showed unusual kindness and their leader, Publius, was the picture of hospitality. I am also inspired by a woman named Nympha whose one-line mention in Colossians 4:15 tells us that Paul wanted to greet those who met for church at her house. This implies that at the very least she was willing to use her home as a meeting place to further the work of God's kingdom. Are you?

And finally, Noah (Genesis 6:13–22)—My boys want to convince me that he was being hospitable by agreeing to take in two of every creature that he found, just like they attempt to do at our house each summer. Sorry, boys, I don't buy it!

3

Family First

When we think of the word *hospitality*, so often we envision friends, extended family, or even strangers entering our home to be fed, loved, and cared for. But what about our own family members? Are we to think of hospitality as pertaining only to outsiders and not to those with whom we rub shoulders and share living quarters day in and day out? I know this was the case for me for many years—too many, I might add. Factoring in the reality that my journey began with an all-out attempt to impress others, it is easy to see how I so easily fell into this pattern.

For a few years it worked. I had a very agreeable husband who worked many hours a week, pouring himself into the lives of teenagers and their families at the church where we were serving. My life was equally busy. Teaching school, coaching cheerleading, and the many hats I wore at church kept me away from home for the majority of my waking hours. But I did try to use my newly acquired cooking and baking skills to bless others. I'd bake a pie for a family going through sickness or take a casserole to a new couple at church.

Together Todd and I would entertain an occasional guest or two on the weekends. It was then I'd pull out all the stops—perfectly clean house, fresh-cut flowers, and a fancy meal unlike any I prepared on a regular basis. I expended great amounts of energy appearing to be a natural hostess. One would think I cooked this way nightly, paid great attention to detail in my house at all times, and pampered my dear husband on a regular basis.

Hardly.

But as I say, I was able to get away with it for a while. But then something happened. One morning upon rising I discovered it. The stick turned blue.

First comes love, then comes marriage, and, well, you know the rest. Along came three babies in six years. Once those little darlin's could string together their first tiny words into coherent sentences, it didn't take long for them to articulate just what they saw.

"Mommy, who is coming over for dinner?" my then-three-year-old daughter would inquire. Wondering how she knew we were expecting company when I hadn't told her, I replied, "Why do you think someone is coming, honey?" "Because you're making homemade rolls, not the 'whack open' kind. You only do that for company," she chimed.

As they grew, more comments began to emerge. "Mom's burning candles. I'll bet she's having her moms group over tonight." "Homemade blueberry pie! Who's it for?" Hardly ever did they assume it was for them.

As much as I hated to admit it, the jig was up. My kids, who often serve as a painstakingly honest mirror when it comes to my actions, had me all figured out. I was a woman living a double standard. I wanted to minister to—read "impress"—others while at the same time ignoring my own family's need for refreshment.

This was easy to do when our clan consisted of just my husband and me. My Mr. Wonderful is a calm, laid-back kind of guy who on the surface never seemed to need much to make him happy. It was easy for me to gloss over him and his needs, surmising he was happy as long as he had something to eat, clean clothes to wear, and, well, plenty of "horizontal fellowship," if you know what I mean.

But with my kids, it was different. Early on they began to verbalize their displeasure at the great meals I would craft for others, not just when company was coming to our house but when a church member or neighbor had a baby or was going through a crisis and needed a meal brought in. I shudder when I think of the many nights another family dined on piping hot baked lasagna, glazed carrots, homemade rolls, and strawberry cheesecake while my own family had a tasty choice between lunch meat sandwiches or peanut butter and jelly. Shame on me.

Now I have adopted a new rule of thumb. With very few exceptions, if the meal I whip up for my own family can't be the same one or at least equal in "yummyness" to the one I would take to another family that night, then I don't offer to make a meal for said family. Ouch! That can be painful to a people-pleasing, how-does-this-look-to-the-outside-world kind of gal like me.

It has also, however, been a huge blessing. My family no longer feels like second fiddle. They are to be my primary ministry, not the recipients of my leftover goods and goodies. In my mind and my ministry, they are to be foremost, not on the back burner. And true to scriptural admonition, that means my husband comes first.

My husband has shared, after much prodding from me assuring him that I could handle the truth, that he hasn't always been "just fine" with my efforts at serving and pleasing outsiders while leaving him to fend for himself. He has admitted that at times he felt slighted because I was baking a pie for the plumber, some cookies for the carpenter, or a torte for the TV repairman while leaving him to rummage through the cupboards for his own snack.

Ladies, please don't fall into the same trap I did. Our families need to come first as the recipients of our love, creativity, and handiwork. If not, you'll be left living an inverted life at the helm of a resentful brood. Trust me. It's no fun.

So how do you put your family first? Well, it starts not in the kitchen with food for the stomach but in the entirety of your home with nourishment for the soul. While foods lovingly served can help minister to your loved ones, what they need most is to feel a sense of belonging—that they are wanted and welcome. For us, seeing this happen all began with a lesson from our past.

When we were newlyweds, my husband was a youth pastor at a country church in our small central Michigan town. Todd had a detailed strategy for the kind of youth group he wanted to see emerge under his leadership at that church. The number one principle he strove to drive into the kids' hearts and minds was this: In this group we will do all we can to create an atmosphere of love. That means no cliques, no put-downs, no harsh words, no kidding! I remember it seemed like we worked for an eternity to solidify these teens from all walks of life into a unified and loyal group. Kind of hard when you have some who are athletic "jocks," some who prefer the library, and a group of giggling girls whose only interest was the latest shade of lip gloss. But what the world's system often can't do was accomplished, in time, in our youth group. They were a team, a collection of individuals that operated as one. We weren't looking for uniformity—all looking and behaving the same way—but for unity. And unity God brought. Those kids stuck up for each other and stuck together. It was a delight to behold.

Our family is diverse too. My husband is the fastidious, some-what serious dad who likes lots of down time and is energized by being alone. I am the fun-loving and fun-instigating mom who tends to let my life get so busy I can't breathe. I am most energized by being with people. Our oldest son, eleven-year-old Mitchell, is an out-of-the-box, methodical thinker who is constantly invent-ing a new way to do an old thing. He is energized by using his brain. "Don't bother me now. I'm figuring!" he used to declare even as a toddler. He also is a clean freak, and we affectionately refer to him as "Neat Nick." Unfortunately, he shares a bedroom with his younger brother, "Sloppy Joe."

Our eight-year-old, Spencer, is the family clown. He plays hard, then drops whatever he is doing—literally—and moves on to the next thing. He is energized by activity and fun.

Our teenage daughter, Mackenzie, is a social creature. An "artsy-smartsy" type, she loves to sing, to create, and above all to talk—whether with her mouth or her hands, as she is fluent in American Sign Language. She is most energized by anyone who will answer back.

Throw us five together on a family vacation and what will you get? A father and son who want to go camping in the wilder-ness all alone, a mother and son who want to take in every sight there is to see while dashing from one activity to the next, and a teenager who doesn't care what we do as long as she can bring a friend or two along, chatting all the way. Oh my!

With such a diverse family as ours, Satan can easily weasel his way in and tempt us to see our differences as being wrong. We can easily get on each other's nerves, verbalize our pet peeves and displeasure at our different personalities, and basically tear each other apart. We've seen it happen in many families and, sadly, often in our own.

We decided to pull out our old youth group strategy. We called a family meeting, sat the children down, and calmly explained what we thought needed to happen in our family to ensure an atmosphere of love. When we came to the part about no put-downs, again our kids were a mirror. It was ever so gently pointed out to us that I am the queen of cutting comments and my husband is the king of sarcasm. Double ouch! Time for the king and queen to be dethroned!

We vowed as a family to work on speaking respectfully, not cutting down others even in jest, and accepting each other's faults and shortcomings. We also pointed out many of our family members' individual strengths. We explained our long-held theory that any strength carried to an extreme can become a weakness. Yes, Mom is good at talking—she even gets paid to do it—and is rather quick-witted. However, that can easily turn into conversation domination or come out in the form of cutting, not-so-funny comments. (I know some days my family just tunes me out during my long-running speeches and must-hear story details. I think they are hanging on my every word. What they really hear is more like the voice of the teacher from the Charlie Brown cartoon special, "*Wa-wa-wa-wa-wa. . . .*")

So now we reserve the right, all five of us, to call the others on the carpet for rude and cutting comments, even those done in jest, that do not create an atmosphere of love. Are we perfect at it? Hardly! But we see progress. And we as parents have to constantly remind ourselves that so much of parenting is about process and progress, not perfection.

Be "Yes" to Their Person

As a couple, Todd and I are currently working hard on a new concept designed to create an atmosphere of love and a feeling of welcome among our offspring. My friend Cathy Tanana, the wife of former major league pitching great Frank Tanana, spoke at a Mug and Muffin Moms' Night Out that was held at our house last summer. Cathy uttered one phrase that night that has been seared in my mind ever since. She talked about how when it comes to our children, we need to *be yes to their person*. That means that if they are exhibiting a behavior that stems from a part of their personality, you don't criticize their person when correcting their behavior. You constantly affirm who they are as a person—one created in the image of God with many wonderful qualities. Don't pick at the parts of them that are different from you, and never criticize them for who they are at the core.

You'd think Todd and I would have known this already. We spent over a decade listening to troubled teens whose parents just wouldn't accept them for who they were. As a result, they sought out those who would. More often than not, acceptance came in the form of the wrong crowd or a member of the opposite sex, and many of the situations ended in near disaster at best.

We do not want this to be the case in our homes! Our spouses and children should feel that home is a refuge, their place of retreat. My heart breaks when I think of the thousands of kids who do not experience welcome in their own home. What could be a more dreadful feeling? Even though most Christian families don't seek to do obvious harm to the spirit of their children, at times subtle messages are given. Johnny is brighter than Suzy. Jimmy is a better athlete than Tom. How we wish Sarah weren't so pokey! Underlying opinions come to the surface much more than we'd like to admit. We need to break this habit before it does real damage.

The practice of being yes to their person will revolutionize your home, whether it is directed to a child, a spouse, or even a roommate! It gives confidence to the timid, courage to the fearful, and strength to the weak. Look for ways to make this concept a reality.

Fostering Friendliness

I sure hope I am alone in this next admission, but I have a sneaking suspicion that I'm not: sadly, I find it much easier to be nice to complete strangers than to my own flesh and blood. Being a person who for most of her life has been addicted to the approval of others, I rarely let my displeasure show. My temper stays in check with the mailman, the gas station attendant, and even the dentist, whom I hate to see twice each year, for crying out loud! Why is it so easy to snap at my kids, give my husband the cold shoulder, or roll my eyes at the comments of a dear family member but remain friendly with those I meet in public even when they do something that really grinds me?

I fear that many of us live out just such a contradiction in our daily lives. And what pictures are our cherished children depositing into their memory banks? "Mom held it together when the dry cleaners completely ruined her favorite sweater, but she yelled at me for accidentally spilling grape juice on the floor." Oh, friends, this should not be!

My friend Sara Eggerichs (wife of Dr. Emerson Eggerichs, author of *Love and Respect*, a fabulous book on biblical marriage) spoke a phrase in my hearing once that I have attempted to weave into the fabric of my life, although it has been quite a struggle. While wrapping up her talk to a group of moms on the topic of marriage, she gave us this simple admonition: "Ladies, now go home and be friendly in your homes."

Wow! What a straightforward and uncomplicated concept. You'd think it would be relatively easy to live out. Be friendly. You know, like we learned in kindergarten. Smile. Be polite. Don't raise your voice. Give others the benefit of the doubt. A piece of cake, right?

I have found that at times it takes every ounce of my energy to maintain my composure, let alone a friendly attitude. However, it is indeed a worthy goal to be friendly in our homes. How heart-breaking it is when those outside our families are treated with more kindness and respect than those whom God has entrusted to us. Let's vow to be friendly in our homes. If we aren't, how on earth will our families feel loved, wanted, and welcome?

Love in Action

Okay, enough about our attitudes—what about our actions? What are some tangible ways we can offer hospitality to our own family members? Well, for starters, let's think about what we do when we have others over to our house to experience our hospitality.

First, there is the house itself. We try to make it an inviting place; you know, not too messy, for starters. How about your home on a daily basis? Do you let it get to the shambles stage in no time at all and leave it that way until company is a-comin'? Do you take care to provide a pleasant atmosphere for your family even in those ordinary days of life? Or are things like wonderfully scented candles, fresh flowers, and soft background music reserved only for entertaining?

What about the food? I've already admitted my past failure in this area. How about you? When expecting dinner or lunch guests, do you spend lots of extra time in the kitchen turning out a gourmet feast even Chef Emeril would be proud of but fail to put much thought or effort into your family's weekly meals? When was the last time you surprised your brood with a new recipe, some from-scratch fare, or a lavish dessert baked just for them and for no other reason than to show them your love and to make them the objects of your hospitality efforts? Try it this week. You'll be glad you did. Besides, they'll think you're up to something!

Again, in keeping with our thinking along the lines of entertaining others, what else do we usually do for guests that can be transferred over to our own kin? How about the conversation?

Have you ever had others over for dinner or even to stay overnight and put some thought into what the conversation would be like? I know for those to whom small talk comes easily, this may not be a concern. I certainly fall into that category. I love to talk and do it easily and often way too much, if the truth be told! But what if the art of conversation doesn't come easily to you? What are some methods for using conversation with your family that will be heartening to them and not too threatening for you?

I have encouraged women to think of some simple questions about daily life to prompt discussion with their husbands and children. In our own family we have a nightly ritual of asking each family member the same three questions before retiring. "What was your high point of the day? What was your low point? And what can I pray about for your day tomorrow?"

These simple discussion-prompters have been the springboard for many treasured talks at nightfall in our home. They are a way not only to stay connected with what is happening in the lives of our children but also to show them that we care about their activities and their feelings about those activities. They can launch us into laughing fits as they recall a humorous part of their day or drive us to our knees on their behalf as we retrace a painful turn their life took that day.

These questions need not be limited to our offspring only. Use them with your husband, when calling grandma, or occasionally with a member of your extended family or circle of friends. They are a tangible tool for showing you care.

Finding Your Family's Ministry

One blessing that comes from having your priorities straight (family first!) in the area of hospitality is that your family will more readily get in on the act when it comes to using your home as an avenue to bless others. When our own clan feels pampered,

A Life That Says Welcome

spoiled, and encouraged, they are more apt to want to do the same for others. Gone will be the resentment at feeling second fiddle to "real company." And they won't feel you are living a double standard—trying to impress others while neglecting your own family's needs. Your lives together can naturally overflow with the love of Christ poured out on those with whom your life naturally intersects. In other words, you'll be a family with a mission!

So often in the corporate world and even the Christian realm, we hear of the importance of having a mission statement. We are told it helps to clarify our purpose, to unify our focus, and to give us a grid with which to sift everything we do. Perhaps the time has come for families to have mission statements too!

Think about the ways God has gifted your family. Are you known for your laid-back lifestyle and always-room-for-one-more attitude when eating or enjoying some good old family fun? Are you mighty in prayer—a family who remembers your church family, pastoral staff, and missionaries as you approach the throne of God? Is your family gifted in the area of ministering to college students or foreign exchange students far away from home? What about some of the more difficult arenas—can you communicate with the deaf, love the mentally challenged, or cater to the needs of the physically afflicted? How does God want your particular family to be his hands and feet to a lost and dying world as well as his mouth speaking words of encouragement to your fellow believers? Talk as a family about how you can articulate your desire to use those gifts by writing a mission statement for your family. It all starts with being willing to use whatever gifts, abilities, and resources God has given you to love and serve others.

"But my husband isn't a believer!" you say. Or perhaps he is, but this hospitality thing isn't quite up his alley. What do you do if you are alone in your desire to open your home up to others?

Hold tight, dear one. Later on we will be discussing ways to offer hospitality "on the road" as well as in your home. Just be assured that God knows your situation and sees your heart. If you picked up this book out of a desire to develop the practice of hospitality, he will provide you with creative ways to do it. Pray. Trust. Believe. And brainstorm! (The last one doesn't sound overly spiritual but has often been the exact place where God has met me most!)

So remember, when it comes to hospitality, family first, please! Focus your time and energies on making those closest to you sense your desire to be one who displays the love of Christ through her attitudes and actions. Don't jump ahead of yourself and try to win the entire town to the Lord when you haven't even made your own spouse and children feel loved, wanted, and welcome. Little things. Small remembrances. Baby steps. Remember, "Whoever can be trusted with very little can also be trusted with much" (Luke 16:10). Keep plugging away with the little. The much will take care of itself.

☙Welcome Ideas❧

Bring Back the Family Table

When it comes to mealtime, try to make the atmosphere at the table pleasant. Serving a family meal on a table that is full of junk mail and clutter or plastered with sticky peanut butter and jam residue from days ago is not a way to say "Welcome!" to your family. Make the table a simple but pretty place. Clear it off, wipe it down, and take a little care in your table setting. I'm not talking fine china here—although once in a while pulling out all the stops for no one else but your family is a sure way to make a memory! Besides the necessary plates, cups, and cutlery, light a candle. When I first started doing this for my family, of course they wanted to know who was coming for supper. Now we often light a candle for no reason at all. It is a simple way to turn an ordinary meal into something a bit more special. (And it has a way of helping kids behave at the table!)

Use family mealtime to catch up on each other's day. How sad it is that often our kitchens serve as nothing more than a family refueling center as each one grabs prepackaged fare and pops it into the microwave and then into his or her mouth before heading out to yet another activity! Make it your aim to have that scenario play out less often. As often as you can, dine as a family. The family table can be a powerful connecting tool. And it doesn't need to be a long, drawn-out affair. Families today are busy. But we certainly can choose a time when most will be home and have a meal that can be enjoyed while chatting over one's day or coming evening activities.

To ensure that mealtimes don't overload Mom, divide up suppertime duties. Mom doesn't need to be the one who sets the table, cooks and serves the meal, clears the dishes, wipes the table, and then finally sweeps the floor! How many years I spent doing all of those very things! Now I know better. A mom with any children over the age of five in the house who doesn't divvy up mealtime duties has only herself to blame!

Occasionally throw some fun into the mundane. Pancakes with Mickey Mouse ears or in the shape of the Batman sign elicit squeals of delight from kids. Simply "draw" a shape as you pour your batter onto the griddle. You can also pour the batter in a letter of the alphabet. Let it cook a minute and then pour more batter on top to make a traditional pancake circle. When you flip the pancake, the letter will stand out. Fun!

Use ketchup to make a heart on their hamburger, or write a message with mustard on their hot dog. I even use a ballpoint pen to write love notes to my husband on the banana he takes to work in his lunch!

Around the House

Beyond mealtimes, there are other simple ways to spread kindness in your home. Try some of these:

Say it with flowers. Did a member of your family have a triumph today? Aced the spelling test, won the ballgame, or landed a part in the school play? Honor them with fresh flowers on the family table. You don't need to drop a bundle of money at the florist. Many grocery stores have small bouquets for under five dollars. Search out secondhand or thrift shops for a lovely vase. Use it again and again as you say "way to go" to family members, honoring them for their achievement or for no reason at all—just because they are part of your family!

Deck the walls. Consider purchasing a whimsical or nostalgic looking chalkboard. Hang it in a prominent place, perhaps the family room or dining or kitchen area. Write messages on it to encourage the members of your household or to remind the rest of the bunch who needs prayer for a particular concern that day. Sometimes use it to write a Bible verse on, keeping God's Word ever in front of your family. We have used a chalkboard near our family table for many of these ideas. Often guests comment on what a great idea it is and then run off to buy their own chalkboard. You can also use it to welcome others who are visiting your home. When a guest arrives and sees "Welcome Aunt Erin and Uncle Bo! We love you!" it will touch their heart.

Put it in writing. Get into the habit of leaving little notes for each other to serve as a pick-me-up. It takes less than a minute to jot a quick sentiment to a family member and then tuck it somewhere where it is sure to be discovered—on a dresser or a nightstand, in a backpack or briefcase. My own kids often use their spare change to purchase a candy bar or little dollar store trinket for another member of the family. Attaching a simple note to it, they'll leave it out for a parent or sibling to discover. We've seen this practice be the means to end an argument, ask for forgiveness, or mend fences between siblings.

Start a parent-child or sibling-to-sibling journal. My friend Wendy Woodruff sparked my interest in this as she told me about a journal she and her teenage daughter keep between them. The concept is this: Purchase a journal to be used between two people as a means of getting to know each other better. Take turns asking a question or putting forth a discussion prompter. For example, Mom writes to her daughter, "Tell me your earliest memories of our first home. What did the various rooms look like? What can you most remember doing in each of the rooms? What do you remember about our backyard?" She then leaves this out for her daughter, who writes several paragraphs giving her answers. Then before giving it back to Mom, she flips the page and asks her own question, like, "Mom, tell me about when you first met Dad. What specifics can you remember? When and how did you know he was 'the one'?" She then leaves it out for her mom, who answers and starts the process all over again. The same concept can be used between siblings who are old enough to communicate by written word. And no, spelling doesn't count!

Make a mural. My friend Jodi Antrim has created an interesting family spot she calls "The Gathering Room." After taping a large piece of butcher block paper to the wall, she shined a spotlight on a family member and traced their silhouette on the paper. She then cut out the pattern, traced it directly on the wall, and painted it a dark, solid color to look like a shadow. Says Jodi, "On the wall is the image of our three-year-old granddaughter. She loves to sing and entertain, so we had her holding a microphone. I just love how it turned out! I walk downstairs and immediately feel as if she's here with me even though they live three and a half hours away."

Display your faith. Jodi also offers another idea I love. In her home she displays a "Wall of Faith." She says, "I went with the idea of having a 'faith wall' of things that mean something to me in my faith journey. I've gathered items such as the photo taken in our sanctuary when our daughters were baptized; a favorite Scripture passage framed; I even have an old walnut hymnal holder and hymnal that were on the back pew of our old sanctuary. It even has the place for the communion cups. I have the little dress I was baptized in, and I'm considering putting that in a box frame to hang. These are the very things that are personal and I think will prompt conversation. Instead of a 'Hall of Fame' it's a 'Wall of Faith.'"

Set up shop. To help facilitate fondness between family members, consider starting your own secret stash of trinkets and treasures that family members may purchase from you for each other. My husband's mother started this Ehman tradition years ago, calling her stash her general store. I have carried this into our own little family. In a large, plastic, colored tub I keep items I have found on clearance racks, in markdown bins, or at resale and thrift shops. I purposely choose items I know various family members would enjoy. When a child or adult wants to "buy" a gift for a family member from "Mom's general store," they may do so. They simply need to perform a small household task, or sometimes I offer them something for free. I will pull out only a few items I think the recipient would enjoy so they don't see items for other family members also inside that big bin. Then they may place the item on the family member's bed or dresser or even in their lunch pail. What a simple way to facilitate family friendliness! (You can also have another bin or two for items family members may give to friends and relatives outside of your home. It especially helps to stock up on a few age-appropriate gifts for the many birthday parties they are sure to be invited to.)

Sing 'em a tune. Music has a way of making wonderful memories. Even if your family isn't melodiously inclined, include music in your everyday life. Play praise music on Sunday mornings as you are readying yourselves for the worship service. Soft instrumental music makes a wonderful backdrop for dinnertime. Let family members take turns choosing what CDs will be played during drive times. Or make your own music! Play the piano or pull out Mom or Dad's old high school instruments and see if you can still play a few bars of your old fight song. At bedtime, sing one verse of a hymn or chorus as you tuck each child in bed. This practice will help to solidify wonderful biblical truths in their minds. This is not just for little ones. Teens still need to be tucked, you know. When the lights are off, they somehow open up. Guaranteed every time!

Time for tea. My friend Teena Sands has a wonderful way to offer hospitality to her girls on a Sunday afternoon. Around 3:00 she puts pink lemonade in a garage sale teapot, sets the table with a couple pink depression glass cups and saucers, and serves a simple sweet (warm muffins, cookies, banana bread). While they eat, she reads a book aloud to them. This has also turned into a good time to talk about things. They might even pick a few flowers from their flowerbeds and add a lit candle to decorate the table. This is one of Teena's favorite things to do with her daughters, and she hopes these tea parties will create lasting childhood memories.

When Comfort Meets Food

Have you ever noticed how the concepts of love and good ol' home cookin' are connected in our phraseology? "The way to a man's heart is through his stomach" and "Nothing says lovin' like something from the oven." Maybe the folks who coined these phrases were onto something!

How many of us can remember cookies baked fresh from grandma's oven or a fresh berry pie cooling on the counter? Do you remember the joy, the anticipation of something delicious to eat? Why in our day have we lost the connection? Is it our ever-busy schedules? Our lack of baking, canning, and cooking know-how? Our assumption that "homemade" is an old-fashioned notion? Perhaps a little of all of the above.

Those in the scented oil and candle business have not forgotten. Have you noticed some of the popular scents these days? Grandma's Oatmeal Cookies. Fresh Baked Cinnamon Roll. Homemade Apple Pie. Why are these such sought-after scents? Their very aromas transport us back in time. Did you know that of all our five senses, smell is the one that is most attached to our memory? Think about it. Haven't you ever gotten a whiff of a scent and instantly thought of someone or something from your past? To this day, if I pass a woman wearing Jovan White Musk perfume, I am suddenly twelve years old again, sitting on my Aunt Patty's sofa while she is brushing the tangles out of my hair.

So why not make similar memories for our own families? Yes, burn beautifully scented candles. But be safe. I like to set a timer for an hour or so to remind myself to blow it out. Be careful blowing it out too. One woman I know blew out a jar candle on her kitchen table as she left one afternoon to run errands. When she returned a few hours later, she found her kitchen engulfed in flames. Seems a small part of the still-burning wick was blown onto her table runner, where it smoldered and then caught her kitchen curtains on fire! Invest in a candle snuffer. They are a bit safer.

While candles add to the atmosphere with their enjoyable scents, they are but imitations of the real deal—lovingly prepared foods. Unfortunately, an entire generation of children is growing up without memories of homemade, from-scratch foods. One worker in a large day care lamented, "These kids, when they play, just mimic what they see on a day-to-day basis. None of them uses the oven when playing in the play kitchen area. They microwave everything!" Let it not be so in our homes!

There are no cookie-cutter molds here (pun intended) when it comes to delighting your clan with a fresh-baked snack. Tailor make your creations to your family's liking. Are you a chocolate-loving bunch? Brownies cooling on the counter waiting to be cut say love to your family. Do you all like your cookies crisp or chewy? Find some fabulous recipes for either kind and make them. (Or to be ahead of the ball game, carve out a chunk of time to freeze up several batches of cookie dough, either in logs wrapped in cellophane or individual balls made with a small metal scoop. *Voila!* Instant fresh-baked cookies. Just add a minute or two to the recommended baking time.) Are you a family full of fruit fanatics? Purchase several pounds during peak season from a local farm market or orchard and freeze some to be enjoyed year-round. (I still remember my brother and me popping frozen, dark sweet cherries into our mouths for an icy afternoon snack.) Are you a staunch proponent of wholesome treats? Whip up a batch of your best whole grain honey-oat granola bars. Anything goes—as long as it speaks love and care to your family.

Creative In-Home Family Dates

Resurrect the practice of having some homegrown family fun. Not the fast-paced, Hollywood kind. The simple, stay-at-home-and-bond kind. Here are some ideas to get you started:

Get board. Be a card. Hold a family night of fun centered on a board game or round or two of cards. It can be a new variety such as Texas Hold 'Em. Or perhaps you'd enjoy a retro round. Many old favorites like Monopoly or Life can be found in new editions. Better yet, try an online auction such as eBay to locate an original. Pop some popcorn; make root beer floats or healthy fruit smoothies. Laugh and play together. (Okay, I'll be truthful: And you'll occasionally fight. You know, Dad plays out of turn, someone accuses little sister of cheating. It doesn't matter! You'll still be making lasting memories.)

Take a walk down memory lane. Occasionally get out the home movies and watch them as a family. Or look at photos from the past. Talk with your children about the way God was working in all of your lives at the time. Help to point your kids to the Author of life who ordained every one of their days even before any of them came to be.

Enjoy your own backyard. Make use of your yard, no matter how small. Serve breakfast on the deck or porch. Pick flowers from your flowerbed for a centerpiece. Play a family yard game such as croquet, horseshoes, or badminton. Blow bubbles. Have a water balloon fight. Spread a blanket out on the ground on a clear, starry night and look for various constellations. Fireflies in a jar, anyone?

Hold a kiddy café. Let the kids (when old enough) plan, prepare, and serve a meal. With the exception of the grocery shopping, Mom and Dad must not be involved! Let them make decorations or arrange a centerpiece. Put on your finest attire and take in a meal at the Kiddy Café. Don't forget to leave a generous tip.

Read. Start the tradition of reading aloud as a family one night a week. It doesn't have to be forever. Try the summer or the month of January. Choose a classic, a mystery, or a book from your childhood. We just finished reading *Charlotte's Web* using the very book my husband had read to him in the 1960s.

Take a hike. Grab a book from the library on plant identification and head out to a nature center or park with nature trails. See how many different plants you can identify.

Create a campfire. Make a bonfire in the backyard or other appropriate place. Roast hot dogs. Make old-fashioned s'mores. Or soak corn in the husks in water for an hour or so and then roast them on a grate over the fire. Let them cool to the touch. Then shuck the ears. Butter, salt, and enjoy! What fun family memories!

Combine your efforts. Collaborate on a homemade family snack before enjoying a television show or movie. See below for some easy and yummy ideas.

Sweet Eats and Sassy Snacks

Here are some simple family snacks that are sure to please!

Orange-cream smoothies. Just like the expensive ones at the mall! Combine 12 ounces frozen orange juice concentrate, 2 teaspoons vanilla, 20 ice cubes, 2 cups milk, and 1 cup sugar in a large blender. Blend until smooth and creamy. Serves 6.

Homemade hot cocoa. Skip the mix and make your favorite mug-filler from scratch. In a large saucepan combine 1 cup sugar, ⅔ cup water, ½ cup cocoa powder, and ¼ teaspoon salt. Heat over medium heat until mixture boils. Boil 1 minute, stirring constantly. Add 8 cups whole milk and heat thoroughly, but *do not boil*. Remove from heat. Add 1-½ teaspoons vanilla or 1 teaspoon almond extract. Top with marshmallows or whipped cream. Serve immediately.

The layered look. Make a layered bean dip using your family's favorite Mexican eats. Try a large platter or pie tin layered with refried beans, taco meat, shredded lettuce, chopped tomatoes, sharp cheddar cheese, salsa, sour cream, and guacamole. Serve with hearty corn tortilla chips for dipping. Blue corn chips are fun!

Stuff it! Making your own stuffed-crust pizza is a snap. Simply make your favorite homemade crust, doubling the recipe to be sure you have enough. Roll the dough out about three inches larger in diameter than your pizza pan or stone. Lay pieces of mozzarella string cheese around the edges of the pan. Fold the excess dough up and over the cheese and pinch down to seal. Prebake crust for 5–7 minutes at 425 degrees. Remove. Add sauce and topping and finish baking, about 5–10 minutes longer. Yum!

Get corny. There's nothing like the smell and taste of homemade caramel corn. Preheat oven to 200 degrees. Make 15 cups popcorn. Mix with 2 cups mixed salted nuts. Spread on lightly greased cookie sheets with edges. Mix 2 cups packed brown sugar, 1 cup real butter, ½ cup corn syrup, and ¾ teaspoon salt in a large saucepan. Cook and stir over medium heat till boiling and bubbly, about 12 minutes or more. Cook 5 more minutes, stirring constantly as mixture maintains a boil and until it forms a soft ball when a small portion is dropped in cold water. Remove from heat. Add ½ teaspoon baking soda. Stir until foamy. Pour over popcorn mixture and stir until well coated. Bake for 20 minutes. Stir and bake 20 more minutes. Remove. Spread on wax paper to cool.

☯ 4 ☯

Cleaning and Clutter, Dustballs and Dirt

God has granted me the precious privilege of spending time with many women's groups throughout my speaking travels. It never ceases to amaze me how, although we live in different communities, attend various churches, and come from every end of the cultural spectrum, in many ways we are so very much alike. As I have spoken on the topic of hospitality, I have been approached afterward by dear sisters who want to offer an idea or ask a question. More often than not, what they really want is a dose of encouragement to get over their fears and apprehensions about opening their homes to others. Because I was hearing the same things from scores of women, I decided to begin taking a formal survey. I really wanted to know two things: First, what are the most common reasons (or should I say excuses?) that women don't more readily open their homes to others on a regular basis?

And second, what are some aspects of being a guest in someone's home that truly are important to people?

Hands down, the most frequently voiced reason these dear gals were hesitant to open their homes to others was the concern that it might not be clean enough. Especially for the audience I most frequently speak to—young moms—they felt it was a hopeless cause. As soon as their house was semi-picked up and relatively clean, along came a little person to mess it up again!

Well, fear not! You can begin to climb out from under the clutter, dig out from beneath the dirt, and finally have this area of your home life under control. Now, I will not guarantee you will have perfection. Far from it. Remember, we are not going for picture-perfect magazine standards. You'd be defeated before you even began. And besides, when it comes to feeling welcomed and refreshed when visiting someone's home, let me tell you what the gals who took my survey said. On a scale of 1 to 10 (with 1 being totally unimportant and 10 being very important), the preference for a home to be spotless got a rating of 2.1. People aren't expecting perfection! What did matter to them was this: that the home was reasonably clean and clutter-free. That received an 8.7.

You see, we may think others are looking for spotless homes and rooms that rank right up there with those on HGTV, but what our guests really desire is a home that is well kept and devoid of a lot of clutter. I was actually surprised at the comments I received in this area. Although I am not a dyed-in-the-wool clean freak who enjoys deep cleaning on a daily basis, I do lean more toward being a Neat Nancy than a Messy Mary. I thought my expectations would be a little stricter than the general population. Not so! Many women asserted just how hard it is to visit with someone when the room is full of clutter—dirty laundry, junk mail in need of being tossed, bills waiting to be paid, dishes that are undone. So we need to come up with a system to keep our clutter at bay so we can actually get to the very surfaces that need to be cleaned! So gals, get ready. Roll up your sleeves. Grab your garbage cans and mopping buckets and make a date with Mr. Clean. We're going to tackle this one head-on!

Kick Out the Clutter

For many households, no cleaning can happen until the clutter is gone—really gone, not just shuffled to another location. But where do we start? With a good old-fashioned dejunking, that's where. This concept has become a regular practice for my husband and me over the past twenty years, but my earliest training came from my mom, whose basic plan of attack was to lock teenaged me in my untidy bedroom with instructions not to come out until it was clean! Oh, how I remember the discouragement I felt as I faced an overwhelming pile of clothes, magazines, LP records (yes, I'm *that* old!), and other assorted kid clutter. My only motivation was my stomach. I wanted to get finished by supper. So I had to become skilled at how to attack my out-of-control room.

I remember sorting items into piles—records here, books there, stuffed animals and dolls in a laundry basket. Then, as if working on a puzzle, I would set about putting those items back where they belonged. All the while the center of my room held the most important organizing tool—a waste basket so I could pitch what was no longer needed, like school papers, *Tiger Beat* magazines, JCPenney newspaper ads. Once the trash was taken out and the objects were back in their rightful places, then I could actually "clean my room" with window cleaner, wood polish, and our trusty vacuum cleaner.

Now that I am a seasoned homemaker, I realize that all those years ago, I had been on the right track. I kept up that simple system through four years (and four roommates) of college and carried it into my marriage . . . well, uh, sort of.

As a new bride I fell into a lifestyle of extreme busyness. I was substitute teaching all day, coaching cheerleading after school, and then swinging by a fast-food joint to pick up dinner for my youth pastor hubby and me as I met him in his office at our church. There we wolfed down our burritos or burgers before attending a meeting. Some nights it was junior high youth group. The next night choir practice. Yet another evening senior high youth group or a business meeting. You get the picture. No time to keep house. We were only home long enough to refuel, re-dress, and go. Our weekends were an even greater flurry of activity. This left me with little time to straighten and clean, and we often lived out of laundry baskets. We needed the clothes long before I could find time to fold them and put them away!

One crisp fall afternoon when I was home for a rare short stint before heading off to an evening church activity, the phone rang. Todd was calling from work to say that a childhood friend of the family was passing through our town and had stopped in to see him at his office. He was just getting ready to come home for a quick bite to eat, so they decided she was going to follow him home to see me and our quaint, modest apartment.

Yikes!

I begged him to delay her as long as he could, reminding him of what the house had looked like when we'd both dashed off to work that morning. Unfortunately, you could take a rather thorough tour of our small town in no more than fifteen minutes! What was Todd to say? "Let's swing down this street once more. Perhaps you didn't get a good glimpse of the post office."

I had no time to lose. I quickly took inventory of the assorted junk that lay around our tastefully decorated but horribly cluttered one-bedroom bungalow. There was only one thing to do: *hide the junk!*

And hide it I did. Into the dishwasher went scores of unrinsed dirty dishes, boxes of crackers, bags of chips, junk mail from the kitchen table, and crusty pots and pans. I quickly shoved all of the clean yet unfolded and stray dirty laundry under our bed. I rushed around the house grabbing anything else I could that was out of place and lying on the floor. For these items I chose our small storage closet off of the dining area as the perfect hiding place. I prayed the doors wouldn't bulge open.

I hastily sprayed some apple cinnamon air freshener into the air as I spun around, opened the door, and exclaimed, "Laura! How nice to see you. Do come in!"

I'll never forget the look on Todd's face as she toured our little place. He tried to disguise his amazement, but occasionally when her back was turned, he'd shoot me a perplexed "Where did all the junk go?" look. We still get a honk out of it today.

After that near fiasco (luckily she never did open a closet or cupboard to check out how much storage space we had), I vowed to get my clutter under control and come up with a cleaning routine that would work for me. Many books and resources I have pored over since then have given me further ideas in this area. If you want more in-depth direction on decluttering, cleaning, and maintaining a clean house, I suggest you track down some of the books in the recommended reading list at the end of this chapter.

Our family now faithfully follows a system of dejunking that we do twice a year. Our biggest dejunking time is the week between Christmas and New Year's when we are taking down holiday decorations and putting away the new toys, clothes, and other assorted goodies we all received. We also do the same thing near the third week of August in an attempt to get ready for the school year ahead. This semi-annual practice ensures that our unwanted junk is weeded out on a regular basis instead of taking up residence in our home, causing us clutter anxiety and preventing us from feeling that we can open up our residence to others. It can work for you too. Here's how.

Dejunking basics: Before beginning, you'll need to gather a few tools to be used in the attack. First, you'll need five boxes or laundry baskets, labeled as follows:

ঌ Put Back

ঌ Take Back

ঌ Toss

ঌ Charity (or Garage Sale if you plan on having one)

ঌ Nostalgia

And, if you are a family who recycles, you'll also need a recycle bin (or another box labeled for recycle if you don't have a bin).

Inside the Put Back box, you will also want to have a smaller container for small things such as pens, paper clips, and small toys. A shoe box with a lid works well. You'll also find it handy to line the Toss box with a trash bag. That way when it gets full, you can simply tie up the trash bag, take it to the garage, line the box with another bag, and keep going!

You'll also find it useful to have your favorite snack and hot or cold drink on hand. Stopping every once in a while for refreshment helps keep your momentum. I also highly recommend the buddy system. Junk clearing seems easier with someone who can help you to think objectively about what you will keep and what you'll toss, give away, or sell. They can help you hang tough when your Tupperware Velveeta Cheese container or that infomercial slice-and-dice gadget you have never used are calling your name.

In fact, in my circle of friends, we have what we affectionately refer to as Amazon Women days when two or three of us get together at one gal's house and help her tackle a nasty chore—such as dejunking, stripping wallpaper, or reorganizing the storage in the basement or garage. The guys keep the kids and have pizza and pop—we dine on Lean Cuisine frozen dinners, chocolate, and cappuccino (they cancel each other out, you know). If you'd like to start this tradition, take turns so every few months it is someone else's chance to have the Amazon Women come to her rescue. If the group approach doesn't work for you, just one friend (or husband, if he's game) will do.

Before embarking on your dejunking journey, review the number one rule of thumb: *if we haven't used it, needed it (but couldn't find it), worn it, or enjoyed looking at it in the past year—then we're going to LET IT FLY!*

Take your boxes into one room of your house. Choose an easy room that is the least cluttered, perhaps a bedroom. Set the boxes in the middle of the floor. Take a deep breath. Start in one corner of the room, pick up an item, and ask yourself these questions:

- *Is this out of place?* Place it in the Put Back box or, if it is a small item, in the shoe box with lid.
- *Does this not belong to anyone in our family?* Put it in the Take Back box. While running errands around town or when heading to church, grab your Take Back box and return those borrowed items!
- *Is it in such dire shape that it is no longer usable?* Then put it in the Toss box that has been lined with a trash bag. But also ask *Is it made of glass, paper, or plastic?* If so, place it in the recycle box (or bin if you have one).
- *Is it in fine shape but no longer needed by anyone in our family?* Into the Charity or Garage Sale box it goes. If time allows, price sale items now to be really ahead of the ball game. If you are donating your items to charity, as the box fills, seal it up and place it in your car so that the next time you are out and about you can drop it off at the local Goodwill or

Salvation Army. Be sure to call ahead to ask for their hours of operation and any guidelines they may have. Don't forget your donation receipt for tax purposes.

❧ Now here is the tricky one: *is it no longer needed by anyone in our family, but one of my children (or my husband) is so attached to it that if I pitch it now, they'll be emotionally damaged for life and, yes, someday they will be on national TV spilling their guts to Dr. Phil about my cruel actions?* Then into the nostalgia box it goes. Each child can have a few nostalgia boxes with favorite "keeper" items. Attach a note to the item such as "You clutched this bear all through your first trip to the dentist" or "You wore this dress on your first day of Sunday school. Your teacher was 'Grandma' Alma Davis."

If the item passes all the tests and is still in your hand, feel free to put it back down where it belongs.

Continue making a circular sweep around the room, picking up more items as you go and following the same steps laid out above. Periodically empty out the boxes—put back the out of place items, throw out the trash bags, transfer the storage and nostalgia items to a box that can be placed in permanent storage, and *keep going*! You can do it! Don't forget to stop for a bite or sip if you need to. And if you are alone, put on some music you enjoy or listen to a book on tape to help pass the time.

You may want to break this task down into bite-sized chunks, especially if your home is overly cluttered. If you can't possibly make a big dent in your clutter over a long weekend, then just tackle one room per weekend.

Now, this will be a huge undertaking the first time you do it. Your house didn't become this cluttered in a day, and it won't get organized in a day either. Especially if a pack rat lives at your house.

A Life That Says Welcome

Our fifteen-year-old, Mackenzie, used to save everything (though she is much better now) and would often attach a sentimental meaning to it—even if it was a bottle cap she found on a hike with her brothers or a menu from a restaurant that her Papa Pat took her to. She was often reduced to tears when we dejunked her room. So we came to an agreement. Occasionally when she was gone, I'd make a clean sweep through her room, tossing anything I deemed as junk into a black garbage bag. When she returned home, I'd announce, "Kenzie, I dejunked your room. If you can tell me anything that is missing, I'll fetch it out of this bag, and you may have it back." It only happened once. Seems I pitched what I thought was a toilet paper tube with tissue stuffed into it. Turns out it was a holder she'd crafted for the tokens she received from her orthodontist for good brushing habits. Well, I never!

Okay. Raise your right hand and repeat after me. "I, (insert your name), do solemnly pledge to stop letting so much junk creep into my house in the first place!" Where does it come from? Does it multiply in the night? Or does it come from others who are sure that their junk is going to be a huge blessing to you? Learn to play defense at the back door with all the well-meaning people who insist on giving you their "stuff" or that awful combination many moms tell me exists in their family: a grandma and the dollar store! I'm just certain that the dollar store was invented by some darlin' grandma who wanted to give her grandkids more stuff!

Speed Cleaning

House dejunked? Boxes emptied out? A place for everything and everything in its place? (Granny would be proud!) Chocolate and coffee consumed? Well, sweet ladies . . . it is time to clean.

I am indebted to my dear friend Suzy for this next idea I have for you. She introduced me to a concept that totally revolutionized my weekly cleaning back in the early nineties. You see, this is the area that threw me for the biggest loop when I became a mom—cleaning!

People used to say about me "You can eat off her floors." Well, after I had a couple of kids in tow, they could still say about me (with a look of disgust) "You can eat off her floors" because there are two meanings to that phrase. Either your floors are so clean you can eat off of them, or so much food has fallen on them that you could easily sit down and have yourself a smorgasbord!

Well, Suzy told me about a book she had purchased that explained a method for cleaning well and cleaning fast. The book is *Speed Cleaning* by Jeff Campbell and the Clean Team. I listened as she described with excitement in her voice how this method had reduced the cleaning time of her four-bedroom farmhouse from an entire afternoon (about four hours) to just under two hours. "And," she added, "my house is so much cleaner than before!" Holy tumbleweeds, Robin! Now she really had my interest.

At the time I lived in a 900-square-foot ranch home. It took me about two and a half hours to clean it well. This was my plan of attack. Thinking myself rather clever, I bought a plastic cleaning caddy and housed all of my supplies in it—window cleaner, wood polish, all-purpose cleaner, and so on. I would situate my caddy in the living room. Then I would proceed to take one cleaning product out of the carrier and walk around my entire house using it on the surfaces it was intended for. First I'd walk around and do all of the windows. Next came all of the wood. Then the sinks and counters. You get the picture. Finally, I'd vacuum and mop. When all was said and done, I had walked the entire perimeter of my house five or six times.

When I borrowed this inspiring and somewhat humorous book from my friend, I realized I had been wasting not only time but a lot of energy and motion as well. The experts at the Clean Team have this all down to a science. They want their professionals to clean as many offices and houses in as little time as possible while still cleaning them better than other cleaning services would. The book helps homeowners to do the same thing. The goal is to help you to save time cleaning so you can spend it doing something you *want* to do.

The main concept that was new to me was the idea that rather than having all of your tools and solutions in a caddy on the floor, you have them in an apron on your body. This way, you can walk the entire perimeter of your house only once, grabbing whatever bottle, brush, rag, or spray you need. Campbell offers his wonderful cleaning aprons for sale on his company's website, www.thecleanteam.com. They are sturdy canvas aprons with multiple pockets and a strong loop on each side to hold your window cleaner and your all-purpose cleaner, which he refers to as blue juice and red juice. In the pockets you have rags, sponges, dust cloths, a toothbrush, a plastic scraper, dusting spray, and so on. Then tucked in your back jeans pocket or in the rear of your apron string you have an ostrich feather duster. Somehow ostrich feathers really attract the dust. Buying a good one is worth the investment. The pastel-colored grocery store ones are made of chicken feathers and only blow the dust around.

Please don't feel that you can't use this system unless you purchase all the products the Clean Team sells. Women have told me that they simply went to a hardware supply store and purchased a canvas apron used by carpenters to hold their nails and tools for less than $2.00. They then sewed a loop of strong cord to each side to hold their spray bottles. Ostrich feather dusters can be found at department stores. You can make your own cleaning solutions. I used many of these same ideas until I could save up enough money to buy the real deal.

So here is how this works. I'll take you through a sample run at my house. Now realize, this is not the time to be picking up junk. This is just a system designed to attack the dirt. We'll start in the kitchen.

I am standing in front of my counter. I pull out my "red juice" and spray, wiping after it has had a chance to work, not as soon as I spray it. If any pie crust residue or peanut butter smears need extra help, I can pull out my plastic scraper to help remove it. I wipe the counter clean. Moving on I come upon my sink. Again I spray, especially around the base of the faucet. I use my tooth-brush to get out the embedded grime from cracks and crevices. I wipe till it shines. If it needs a dose of scouring powder, I have a small shaker of it in one of my apron pockets, along with a sponge. I shake, scrub, and rinse.

Now I encounter my refrigerator. Again out comes my "red juice" and rag. Following one of the Clean Team's thirteen basic rules, I work from top to bottom. (Dirt follows gravity, you know. Working from top to bottom ensures you won't have to clean a surface twice because dirt from above fell onto it.)

Now I'm facing a window. No need to fear; I simply whip out my "blue juice," spray, and wipe. Below the window is a solid wood table. Out of my apron comes my wood polish and cleaning cloth. I spray and wipe until it glows. (A little hint: The Clean Team offers some wonderful 100 percent cotton cleaning cloths that are well worth the investment. However, when I was first starting out, I found that old cloth diapers and slightly worn Fruit of the Looms worked just fine too!)

Now I am in my living room and standing in front of my antique plate rack. It is only slightly dusty. No need for a major clear and clean job. I merely grab my ostrich feather duster from my back pocket and give the rack a light dusting. The dust clings to the duster. I bend my right knee, kicking up my foot to the rear, and then whack the duster on my ankle. The dust falls into the carpet, where it will be vacuumed up later. I keep walking

A Life That Says Welcome

the perimeter of my house, pulling out whatever I need to clean that is before me, always working from top to bottom.

When I am done with a room, I either vacuum or wet mop it, transporting these two items along with me as I go. All the while I am smiling just thinking of the time I am saving and the deep cleaning I am doing. When I am finished, I feel a sense of pride knowing that I have touched nearly every surface in my home on a weekly basis. It makes so much sense to be proactive in our cleaning, giving items a quick wipe or swipe before they have reached the point of no return due to long-term neglect—like once a week rearranging your fridge shelves, throwing out food gone bad, and wiping the shelves clean. You know, *before* you need to use a chisel and wear a hazmat suit because you haven't touched it for three months!

Once I became proficient at the speed cleaning method, my weekly house cleaning went from about two and a half hours to an average top speed of forty-five to fifty-five minutes. My two children, ages two and five at the time, were even in on the act. They would follow me around with an old white gym sock on their hand helping me dust. We'd reward ourselves at the end with a walk to the park or another chapter in our current read-aloud book.

I know many of you are thinking, "This is too much work." You were hoping I'd give you some magical formula and *voila*! Instant organized and clean house. But you know what? Being organized and practicing a workable cleaning routine does take work, but the rewards are so worth it. You may have to get up a little earlier, stay up a bit later—but do you know that is biblical? The woman described in the book of Proverbs, chapter 31, accomplished a great deal but also put the Lord and her family first and was greatly praised for it. And what does it say about her? "She also rises while it is yet night" (v. 15 NKJV), preparing food for the coming day and for her maidservants. I know, I know . . . I'd get up early and fix some vittles if I had the luxury of having maidservants too. Not so fast! We do have servants. They aren't human; they are electric—our appliances. They are designed to do much of what our dear ancestors did while we go on to tackle another task.

Back to Proverbs 31. It is said about her that "her lamp does not go out at night" (v. 18 NKJV). For you that might mean staying up a bit late to finish scrubbing that last pot or to throw in that final load of laundry. (Although my husband has his own interpretation of that verse—he reads it with eyebrows raised and a frisky wink, "Her lamp does not go out at night!" Are you tracking with me, ladies?)

Back to our buckets. The joy of working this cleaning method into your weekly routine is that you will no longer feel that your home is out of control. Yes, toothpaste still splatters in the sink, juice still spills on the floor, and you still have to spot clean little mishaps each day, but your home will no longer be hopelessly filthy because it hasn't had a good cleaning in months. When you cease to fear someone may ring your doorbell while the house is a wreck, you can relax and work on your welcoming skills. Remember, we aren't going for perfection. A friend may stop by while you are folding laundry or when dirty dishes are stacked in the sink calling your name. It's okay! Remember, we are shooting for "reasonably clean and clutter-free," not spotless. That, my friend, you can do. I believe in you! And I've seen other women, including myself, do it.

And please, if you are a mom with young children at home, don't fall into one of two traps that we women can so easily fall into. The first one is the temptation to throw up your hands in complete capitulation and just let the little buggers wreak havoc with your home. It is deciding that you are terribly outnumbered and outwitted and that trying to maintain any reasonable semblance of order is just too tiring. These moms decide to let the house go and let the kids rule. They'll finally clean when the youngest turns eighteen. The result is that the kids learn no respect for the property of others, nor for their own, for that matter. Pity their future roommates and spouses!

On the other end of the spectrum are the paralyzed perfectionists. They are so aghast at the messes that little ones can make that they outlaw any and all kidlike behaviors that might produce any messes. And they refuse to display any items that might suggest that little people are anywhere on the premises. No toys in the living areas—too cluttery. No crafts or paint in the house—too dangerous for carpets and couches. No watercolored masterpieces adorning the fridge—too, well, unstylish. When we behave like this, we make our children grow up in a home that wants to pretend they don't exist, one that shuns displays of childhood and scoffs at the work God has assigned to them—their play!

May I gently suggest that neither of these extremes is the best road to take. (I know. I've tried them both!) The better path is somewhere right down the middle. Embrace your kids and their treasures, but teach them good housekeeping habits. Find creative ways to exhibit their art, to flaunt their flair for the things of childhood, but insist that they take part in the keeping of the home. Teach them boundaries. Insist that they mind them. And for heaven's sake, don't make them feel the need to apologize for simply being a kid! Remember, be yes to their person.

Well, are you up for the challenge to get your cleaning habits—or lack thereof—under control? Spend some time finding your groove, a rhythm of work that helps to banish from your mind that awful feeling of panic that you experience when you hear the doorbell ring.

The tools are here. Just be patient. Give yourself a month or two to make this routine part of your reality. Then put on the coffeepot. Company's a-comin'!

∞Welcome Ideas∞

Eradicating "Packitus Ratimus"

It is a dreadful disease. My mother has it, as does my mother-in-law. Many women their age have been stricken with it. I guess the further along in years you are, the more likely you are to have it. In fact, I've heard that those born during the Great Depression most often have some form of it. All I know is I am determined not to catch it, for I have seen the havoc it can wreak upon a person and the utter torment it can cause their spouse. Funny thing is, they could be freed from it, if they only wanted to. What is this horrible disease? It is called Packitus Ratimus.

Yep, both my mom and my mom-in-law are major pack rats; they can't get rid of anything! While their living quarters are neat and clean and devoid of dirt, their basements and spare closets, well . . . that's where the main clutter culprit lies. And they can reason it away. You see, they just might *need* that old rotary dial phone someday or discover a use for Aunt Tilly's broken-down sewing machine. Yes sir, they anticipate a coming worldwide shortage of empty coffee cans, used margarine tubs, or baby food jars from the 1960s. When it happens, they'll be ready.

I, on the other hand, will take my chances. For some odd reason, both my husband and I are exactly the opposite of our dear mothers. We've determined to keep our household inventory down to the bare minimum. When the April issue of a magazine arrives, the March one is tossed in the recycle bin. We've made a solemn pledge to each other that we will not have six-foot-high stacks of decades-old magazines cluttering our basement, waiting for us to clip out the interesting articles or yummy recipes "someday." It was part of our marriage vows, as was the part about me promising to never carry a purse larger than five-by-seven inches. For Todd it ranked right up there with "to love, honor, and obey." Seems he was emotionally scarred from being known as the kid with "the mom with the gigantic purse." I told him to look on the bright side. I'll bet he was also known as the kid whose mom always had the needed Band-Aid, needle and thread, Scotch tape, or bubble gum readily available at the ball games and band concerts.

Each year we make good on our vows and set aside a few days after Christmas for major spring cleaning. Yes, I know that's not technically "spring," but it's what works for us! As we donate or sell unwanted items and toss or recycle others, we feel such a sense of calm and lack of clutter. Several years running, we have even hosted a garage sale selling our unwanted items, too-small kids' clothing, and no-longer-loved toys. Each spring we have raked in between $300 and $1,000 depending on how many big-ticket items we had.

We do save those favorite "keeper" items our kids are attached to (some of them, at least) instead of sticking a price tag on them. Then they can have these items to pass down to their children. I also saved one baby blanket and the sleeper they came home from the hospital in for each child, something our own pack rat mothers did. These ancient items were a joy for us to use and, luckily for the grandmas, they had a full nine months' notice before they had to unearth them!

After dejunking and before putting the rooms back in order, we do some deep spring cleaning. I scrub walls, clean light fixtures, and wash windows with the help of our little ones. With Q-tips in hand, Todd does the detail work—items and areas with small cracks and crevices. We get such a good feeling when we are done that we can understand why John Wesley said, "Cleanliness is next to godliness." In fact, in other cultures, Poland for example, spring cleaning takes on a spiritual connotation. In the days preceding Easter, they take very seriously getting all of the dirt out of their lives and off of their windows. Spring represents rebirth; the shining sun offers hope; and putting their physical and spiritual lives in order before celebrating the death and resurrection of Jesus is of utmost importance.

So, fellow clutter chasers and dust bunny destroyers, will you stand with me in refusing to join the ranks of the pack rat club? You'll be blessed with a clean house, an uncluttered mind, and maybe even a little extra cash in your pocketbook.

A word of caution, though: make sure your extended family retains one token pack rat. Grandma is best. You never know when your child may bring home a school assignment that begins with the words, "Take one used coffee can . . ."

Homemade Cleaning Supplies

Of course you may buy your sprays and solutions at the store, but if you are concerned about safety and wish to use cleaning supplies that are environmentally sound and don't give off harsh fumes, mix up some solutions yourself from the list below. Or if you'd like to purchase ready-made cleaning supplies that meet these criteria, visit the website of the Clean Team (www.thecleanteam.com) or Melaleuca: The Wellness Company (www.melaleuca.com).

First, make sure your cleaning cupboard has the following components handy, ready to be mixed:

- Baking soda
- Borax powder (found near the laundry soap in your grocery or department store)
- Clear liquid dish soap, such as Ivory brand
- Club soda
- Common table salt

ᴥ Lemon juice

ᴥ Olive oil

ᴥ Regular tea bags

ᴥ White vinegar

Use the above to make the following solutions:

All-purpose cleaner—Mix a quart (4 cups) of water, ¼ cup lemon juice, 1 teaspoon liquid dish soap, 1 tablespoon each of borax and baking soda. Keep in a spray bottle and shake before using. Works great on any hard surface such as counters, sinks, and appliances.

Carpet and cloth stain remover—Simple club soda. Keep this around to quickly apply full strength to any stain you have including blood, tea, coffee, juice, or soda pop. With a clean cloth, blot up as much of the stain as you can. Then generously pour the club soda over the stain until it is well saturated. Blot with a clean rag and repeat the process until the stain is gone.

Dishwasher spot stopper—In a small, plastic, lidded container, keep a mixture of 1 cup borax mixed with ½ cup baking soda. Add 1 teaspoon to each load of your dishwasher, along with your regular detergent.

Shower cleaner—Heat full strength white vinegar on the stove until it is warm but not too hot to pour into a bottle. Place in bottle and spray on shower walls. Let sit for a few minutes, scrub with a sponge, and rinse well.

Sink cleaner—Scrub with a sponge and a paste made from equal parts of salt and baking soda moistened with a little water. Rinse well. To give the drain a good cleaning, pour a generous amount of baking soda down the drain. Next pour a little white vinegar down the drain and let bubble. Throw a handful of ice cubes in and run the garbage disposal for a few seconds.

Rinse well. Finally, shine with a cloth moistened with a little club soda.

Window cleaner—Make a solution of ⅓ cup white vinegar to a quart of warm water. Pour into a clean spray bottle and spray. (For really stubborn outside dirt, mix ⅓ cup ammonia, ⅓ cup white vinegar, and 2 tablespoons cornstarch in a bucket of warm water. Warning: Ammonia does give off harsh fumes. Do not use around children.)

Floor cleaners—Before cleaning any floor, sweep well and scrape up any residue of food or play dough with a plastic scraper. For vinyl floors, clean with a mop or sponge with a simple mixture of one tablespoon of borax to a gallon of warm water. For hardwood floors, brew two regular tea bags in a quart of boiling water. Let cool until slightly warm. Using a mop or sponge, clean the floor and wipe with a clean rag. The tannic acid inherent to the tea makes for a wonderful cleaner.

Furniture polish—For a wonderful polish for real wood surfaces (not imitation or laminate) mix ¼ cup white vinegar with ¾ cup olive oil. Wipe on lightly with a cloth and wipe clean with another. In between cleanings, wipe lightly with a cloth soaked in the wood floor cleaner solution above.

Clutter Control

Once your home is rid of unwanted junk and cleared of clutter, how do you prevent it from getting out of control again so fast? Institute a few household guidelines.

Head junk off at the pass. Don't take anything into your home that you really don't want. If offered your neighbor's leftover garage sale items, politely decline. If Aunt Lucy brings you a box of goodies that you think are no good, donate them to a secondhand store the next time you are out and about. Before purchasing even a small item, ask yourself, "Do we *really* need this? Do I want to spend the time and energy to clean/repair/maintain this gadget or gizmo? Am I sure this won't wind up in a pile of unwanted junk in the near future?" If the answer to any of those questions is no, then don't buy it!

Don't put it down, put it back! Teach even the youngest members of your household to put items back in their proper place once they are finished with them or bring them into the house from school, church, etc. Putting something down "for now" often leads to clutter as these misplaced items occupy territory where they were never meant to be. Even three-year-olds can be taught to put their toys and belongings back "where they live."

Grandma was right—have a place for everything and everything in its place. Know where you will store your stuff and your family's stuff. If you have piles of nomadic notions wandering from room to room, take an afternoon and find places where they will permanently dwell.

Utilize baskets and bins. There are so many functional yet pretty storage containers for sale nowadays. Take a trip to a department store or spend a few minutes online locating some lovely baskets and bins that can do double duty and hide some of your objects.

Get on a roll. Check classified ads in the newspaper to see if you can locate a good used rolltop desk for sale. These are wonderful for organizing your bills, school papers, and such. They come equipped with many drawers, cubbies, and slots that can help to organize your papers. Our family has three: one for our main living room, a small antique one for letter writing that sits in our master bedroom, and one for a teenage daughter's trinkets, treasures, and homework folders. The best feature? If the desk's surface does become messy, you can always roll the top shut.

Give an assignment. Purchase a plastic crate or tote for each child and store in your mudroom or entryway or other

---

appropriate area. When you locate your loved one's belongings in a place they don't belong, place them in their crate. Each person must empty out his or her crate each evening before nightfall.

Set up a junk jail and serve as the parental warden. Any child's item that regularly finds its way out of its proper place and into your way will be promptly confiscated. Offending owners must post bail in order to get the item back. Set an appropriate amount and double the fine if the item is jailed for a second offense. (Works well for messy husbands, too!)

Stairway to heaven. Well, not really to heaven, but this idea can help to bring a little peace on earth. Purchase a stairstep basket designed to fit neatly on your stairs. When you run across upstairs items that really belong downstairs or vice versa, place them in the basket. The key is emptying out the basket every so often, before it is overflowing!

Make a clean sweep. Occasionally set a timer for twenty minutes. Then, toting a box or basket, give a bedroom or living area the once-over, gathering up and putting back any items that have managed to migrate somewhere they don't belong.

Weekly Cleaning Basics

When tackling your weekly cleaning, follow this logical order:

- ᛒ Pick up junk or assign the task to your darling offspring.
- ᛒ Gather all your tools and cleaning supplies and put them in your apron or in a tote you will carry with you from room to room.
- ᛒ Start in the kitchen. Work your way around the perimeter of the room, cleaning from top to bottom whatever surface is before you using the appropriate products and tools.

A Life That Says Welcome

- Keep moving, on to the next room. Follow the same "around the room" pattern. As you come to surfaces that only need a light dusting, dust them with your feather duster and then whack it on your ankle, letting the dust fall into the carpet or on the floor.

- Point to remember: Do you know what are the dirtiest, most germ-infested items in your house? Your doorknobs—because everyone touches them but no one ever cleans them. So before you leave a room, wipe down both sides of the doorknob with a disinfecting cleanser.

- Once the main cleaning is done in each room, sweep or vacuum the floor, and finally damp mop any hard floor surfaces.

- Put your feet up and enjoy a nice drink and a little something to read. Don't feel guilty for lounging. You saved so much time by cleaning your home with logical order and at such top speed!

Age-Appropriate Chores

Don't let your little ones off of the hook when the time to work rolls around. Even mini-munchkins can pitch in to help earn their keep. Here are some age-appropriate chores they can perform.

In the kitchen—Let them help prepare simple foods. They can wash fruits and vegetables. They can chop carrots with a butter knife or learn to carefully use a potato peeler. They can certainly be trained how to set the table or get the needed condiments out of the fridge.

Laundry—Have a different color laundry basket in everyone's closet. Children who are old enough and responsible husbands also get a stain stick. They will stain stick their clothes and on laundry day will take their basket to the laundry room and put the clothes in the appropriate piles—whites, lights, darks, towels. You'll wash and dry the clothes. After they are dry, either put the clothes back in the proper person's basket for them to fold and put away or spread a blanket on the floor, dump all the laundry on it, and play "Friday night find and fold." That's where they retrieve their clothes, fold them, and put them away while you watch a video and have pizza or popcorn.

Your weekly cleaning routine—Dole out duties that can be performed with relative ease. Put an old white sock on their hand and let them dust the furniture. Give them a spray bottle of safe cleaner and assign them the lower glass surfaces to clean (you will need to supervise the first few times). They can certainly sweep, and most kids love to run a vacuum.

Give 'em a green thumb—Even young children can help with the yard work. Teach them what weeds look like and how to pull them. Let them water the flowers or pick tomatoes. They can rake leaves or pick up pinecones. (My own three kids have such fond memories of doing just that for their Grandpa Ehman who is now in heaven. Of course Grandpa's heart was giving and his pockets deep. Each child was paid a penny for each pinecone they found, and they usually found hundreds!)

Let them chip in on chores—They can water plants or get the mail. They can sweep out the garage. They can take the newspapers out to the recycling bin. They can feed the dog or cat. Start now instilling a healthy work ethic in them.

In their own space—Let them know just what *you* think a clean room looks like. Kids' standards of course will not always match ours. They most likely have no idea where to begin or have any idea just what "clean" looks like to Mom or Dad. Don't simply shout, "Go clean your room!" Come alongside them and show them how. I struggled for years with my pack-rat inclined daughter. Often one of us was reduced to tears as I urged, cajoled, and forced her to deal with the clutter, chaos, and confusion that occupied her room. Finally, at my wit's end one day, I decided to actually pray about it. (Why do we sometimes consult the Lord only after all our man-made attempts fail?) He gave me a brilliant idea. Remember the old saying "If you can't beat 'em, join 'em"? I decided to join my daughter that day. Instead of coming down with an iron fist and checking on her every few minutes to see how she was doing, a process that usually took hours and left her feeling belittled, I actually *helped* her clean her room. Novel idea, right? Well, I didn't just *help* her; I did it in her style. I fixed us each a soda pop, put on some of her favorite strawberry-flavored sparkle lip gloss, and gathered my hair into a high ponytail. I entered her room and cranked up her new ZOEgirl CD. She could hardly believe her eyes. We laughed and danced and tossed trash as I showed her, without yelling, what we expected in her room. I did yield to a few compromises. I realized my standards had been too high. Preteen girls have lots of stuff, and it is part of their identity. I had just become tired of viewing her treasures sprawled on her floor, especially since her room is directly off of our living room, in plain view. So we trekked off to the store to purchase some cool totes, baskets, and caboodles to disguise her stuff. Now, four years later, her room is usually picked up and cleaned without any help from me. She knows what is expected and how to get there.

Recommended Reading List

- *Get More Done in Less Time* by Donna Otto. A wonderful resource to refer to again and again. It covers nearly every aspect of organization with clear tips and simple strategies.
- *Cleaning Up the Clutter, More Hours in My Day,* or almost any other book by Emilie Barnes. Her books are chock-full of great, doable ideas and are so inspiring!

- *Speed Cleaning* and *Clutter Control* by Jeff Campbell and the Clean Team. For a free catalog of their helpful products, call 1-800-717-CLEAN (2532) or visit them at www.thecleanteam.com.

- *Is There Life After Housework?* and *The Cleaning Encyclopedia* by Don Aslett—this guy is a pro as well as a complete stitch! You'll laugh your way clean.

- *Talking Dirty with the Queen of Clean* by Linda Cobb. A handy resource for how to clean just about everything that gets dirty!

5

The Myth of the
Too-Small House

Remember now that our little Bible lesson proved that this business of hospitality is not an optional activity. We are expected to use our homes to minister to others and to live a life that says "welcome" to those around us. So why the excuses? Are we lazy? Unmotivated? Embarrassed? Afraid? Or are we simply not willing to trust that God will enable us to do what he has told us in his Word we are supposed to be doing?

When I was on my own and able to use initially my dorm room, then our apartment, and finally our first house as a center of hospitality, it took me awhile to develop the right perspective. I started out seeking to amaze my friends and astonish my new family with my entertaining prowess. I learned quickly that offering hospitality was not about impressing others. Opening your home to others in order to "wow" them with your food or dumbfound them with your décor only leaves you feeling empty, even if said company was indeed "wowed." Our actions must be about a higher purpose than self-seeking.

Additionally, I had to get over the feeling I often got that our little place was just not as spacious or beautiful as others' homes. I felt like we were always just a little bit behind our circle of friends. We were the last ones to buy a home, the last to own a VCR and video camera, and the last to afford a cell phone, for heaven's sake! And I compared our family with those "further down the road financially" families all the time.

Comparisons kill contentment. And my contentment? It was deader than a doornail.

Oh, is this a lesson I have had to learn over and over again in my life as a stay-at-home mom! Living on one income has simply forced us to do without some luxuries and delay buying items that many of our friends and family members obtained long before we ever could. Although Todd and I both agreed that this would be our lifestyle and I simply cherished being the one caring for my kids 'round the clock, many times the results of such a lifestyle had me throwing myself a personal pity party. I would mumble and grumble about not owning a house or, once we owned one, not owning a big or new house. I'd feel second class to those who could afford to decorate beautifully or hire a house cleaner or put in a swimming pool. Sigh.

But God had an important lesson to teach me regarding the true meaning of contentment: *true contentment is not having what you want but wanting what you have.* Let that sink in for a moment.

Being truly content is not just receiving every imaginable heart's desire. That is having what you want. Rather, contentment is wanting nothing more than what you already have. It is a heart that says, That's enough, that's sufficient, that's more than adequate, I have plenty, thank you. Listen to the words of

A Life That Says Welcome

the apostle Paul, who was poor and in prison, without many material trinkets to call his own or a home to own:

> I have learned to be content whatever the circumstances. I know what it is to be in need, and I know what it is to have plenty. I have learned the secret of being content in any and every situation, whether well fed or hungry, whether living in plenty or in want. I can do everything through him who gives me strength.
>
> Philippians 4:11–13

This man of God was able to be truthfully content with his lot in life even though that lot brought him so little. Well, women of God, what about us? What are our current circumstances in life? Do you live in an older, smaller, or not-so-nice home? Got a pack of little ones running behind you messing up your newly straightened home faster than you can say Tinkertoys? Do you run with a crowd that lives an elevated lifestyle that makes you feel like you reside on the other side of the railroad tracks, monetarily speaking? Or perhaps you feel at a loss for just how to do this hospitality thing in the first place and you fear that no one will even want to be a guest in your home.

Perfect. That is just where God wants you, insecurities and all. You see, I didn't write this book just to get you to have an occasional dinner party or entertain an overnight guest. It isn't even meant to merely inspire you to open up your home and your heart to willingly serve others. Oh no, dear sisters. It is about so much more than that! It's all about you and your relationship with God.

The biggest blessing I hope will make its way from this book into your heart is that you will begin to see this process as an adventure. You see, I fully expect you to have a blast with God as you begin to pray seriously and look to him at every step of this hospitality journey. He is willing and waiting to prove to you that whatever he calls you to do, he also equips you to do. And gals, he has called us to be hospitable. I can't wait to stand on the sidelines and smile as the timid begin to welcome in guests, the hesitant commence to reach out willingly, and those who felt they couldn't afford such a lifestyle begin to see God provide all that is needed for them to live a life that says "welcome." Your relationship with others will strengthen and your faith in God will grow as you walk faithfully down the path he has laid out for you.

Your Small World

Now, in order to take the first step down that path, we need to get rid of those excuses! Let's start with one I frequently used to say and now still hear often from women: "My house is just too small."

Oh, really?

Our first home was a small ranch built in the 1950s on a maple-lined, modest street in town. It had barely over 900 square feet of living space with a basement under only about half of the house that could be used for storage. Our kitchen was so small that our kitchen table, while only large enough to seat four when the sides were up and in place, had to have the ends in the dropped-down position to allow us enough space to walk through during waking hours. Once mealtime arrived, we flipped the ends up and locked them in place. Then we pulled it out away from the wall a bit so we could be snugly seated at the table. It actually came in handy. If we needed something from off the stove or out of the fridge, we didn't need to budge. Our backs were up against these appliances when we ate anyway!

When originally built, this home had two bedrooms. A small room off of the biggest bedroom that was added later served us well as a nursery. The house had only one double closet and two that were the size of a small coat closet. The bathroom could only fit one person at a time unless you sucked your stomach in and scooted along.

Yep, it was small, all right. But we loved it! It was a home, our first home. We were owners, not renters, and were able to paint and pound nails into the walls without asking the landlord first! And for two or three years after we moved in, we were clipping along pretty well.

And then we had kids. Three of 'em came along in six years. And all of our friends had kids too. So suddenly, instead of Richard and Suzy and their toddler coming over for dinner, it was Richard and Suzy and our combined eight children under the age of twelve! We just plumb ran outta room.

I was whining on the phone to my friend Suzy about this one day as one of my other friends was moving into her newly built two-story home that had three times the square footage that ours had—and a fireplace to boot!

Unfortunately, my husband overheard me. Mistake number one. (Ladies, if you are going to whine about your home, don't let the mister hear you. Not only do men not like whining in general, but it makes them feel that they aren't providing for the family in a satisfactory manner.)

So after I hung up, my hubby and I had a little chat about our cramped quarters and how it was cramping my hospitality style. I could cite plenty of reasons that it was getting nearly impossible to open our home for meals and such. And in my "holier than thou" way I could name several other Christian families with larger or newer homes who never even had company over at all! It just wasn't fair!

Once I calmed down and began to listen to the voice of truth—my husband's straight shooting—my whining turned to reason. He recounted the stories we'd heard of courageous and charitable Christians around the world. Many of them lived in very small spaces, sometimes twelve people from three generations in a twenty- by twenty-foot space. Do the math. That's 400 square feet! We had five people in over 900 square feet! Suddenly it didn't seem so cramped any longer. And these Christians would gladly open their small abode to church members or guest missionaries even though they had so little to give. Some even saved what they thought was a rare treat such as a package of Kool-Aid or jar of fruit preserves and served it to their company. At the very least, they were delighted to add a few more cups of water to the already simmering soup or stew in order to stretch the meal a bit. Just being reminded of their generosity made me feel utterly ashamed at my behavior.

Right then and there in our minuscule little kitchen, we decided this: we would stop complaining and focusing on what we didn't have. Instead, we would center on what we did have. And cramped or not, we would continue to use our home for the Lord. We decided that if we never were able to move into another larger home, it would be just fine, as long as we maintained perspective—you know, thinking about the whole world and how they live, not just our American neighbors. We also wondered aloud if this was one of those times when God was checking to see if we could be faithful with little before we had a chance to show him we could be faithful with much.

So I made an all-out attempt to try to change my attitude and be thankful for our quaint but cramped place. I admit I still complained at times, but I was careful not to do it in front of Todd! During this time my mother-in-love gave me a book by a woman she had heard speak while wintering in Florida. It was the book *First We Have Coffee and Then We Talk* by Margaret Jenson, the enchanting true story of the family Margaret grew up in. She was the daughter of a preacher and an amazing wife who ministered to Scandinavian immigrants over the course of many decades. Margaret's family lived a life of hospitality as her mother put on the coffeepot and opened her heart to whomever

God brought their way—lumberjacks, orphans, neighbors, and strangers—even though they themselves lived a very modest, unassuming lifestyle on a meager pastor's salary.

Once Margaret was out on her own, she was talking to her mother about feeling that her own place was not big enough to entertain company. It was then that Margaret heard these words from her mother, spoken with true conviction and a thick Scandinavian accent: "Ven there is vroom in your heart . . . then there is vroom in your home."

You see, this dear saint knew what was actually essential in a home. It wasn't space, or a feast, or worldly beauty. It was a heart that had room; one that could put on the coffeepot and put aside the distractions of self and self-consciousness in order to listen and to love. Many years had proved this true for Margaret's mother, and it was a theory I needed to show true as well.

One day while my children were napping and I was baking a batch of muffins in my ever-so-small kitchen, a friend stopped by to drop something off. Not just any friend, mind you. This was the same friend I had been so jealous of earlier that year because she and her husband built that beautiful, big house. After we chatted for a minute and before she turned to leave, she looked around my petite pantry, let out a sigh, and declared, "I just love your house."

Pardon me? Did she just say what I think she said?

"Oh," I replied. "You do?"

She continued, "Yeah. There is just something special about your home. It is always so warm, cozy, and inviting over here. I just love being at your house."

Gulp. *She* loved being at *my* house? Remember now, I *coveted* her home. I discussed this bizarre declaration my friend had made with my husband after he returned home from work that evening. As we thought about it, we decided that God was beginning to show us what we were learning was true: when there is room in your heart, there is room in your home. And the most important thing you need to display in your home isn't a new piece of furniture or a big screen TV; it is the love of Christ. I firmly believe what made my friend fond of our home was the love of God she sensed when she was there. It couldn't have been the spacious living areas or fancy décor, because we had neither! It was the love she sensed as she saw us serve each other and willingly open our place to her, even though I felt a bit embarrassed by its size.

Making Room

Okay, back to our excuse. While it is true that if there is room in your heart, then there is room in your home, it is still helpful if you make as much room as possible in your home so you don't feel it is so cramped and are more able to have company comfortably. So what's a gal to do?

Well, first of all, we need to use our limited space. My little hospitality survey found that the ladies felt that homes are much more inviting when they are clean and clutter free. I hope you have been inspired to dejunk your home and have only the items your family actually needs left within your walls. But let's face it, we still need to store some of our stuff—off-season clothes, clothing that one child has outgrown but another isn't quite into yet, holiday decorations, wrapping paper, craft supplies, and tax returns and other must-keep documents.

Learn to be creative in your storage. For off-season and other clothes, invest in plastic (such as Rubbermaid) boxes, bins, and totes and label them well. One gal told me she uses a china pen to write on the side of the box what its contents are. Then, when the contents of the box change someday, she wipes off the writing and relabels it. Plastic containers such as these are wonderful because they stack well and are waterproof. You also can purchase them in the clear variety so you can see just what is in them.

If you can't afford to buy these containers, check with an office to see if they will save the boxes that computer paper comes in for you. I used these for years, and they worked well and were free. You can label the side of the box or, if you'd prefer, many experts suggest using a numbering system. Simply number your boxes and then keep corresponding index cards that list what items are in that particular box. This way when the contents of the box change, you don't need to cross off what you have written on the side; you just tear up the card and make a new one. My friend Carmen tries to use numbers that are easy to remember. Several boxes labeled 25 have her Christmas items in them, because that holiday falls on December 25. Box number 15 has her husband's deer hunting apparel in it, because November 15 is opening day of firearms deer season here in Michigan—it's a big day for many, and some schools even give the students the day off!

When it comes to room for storage, be resourceful. Go on a space exploration. No, not the "Beam me up, Scotty" kind but a trek to find unused areas for storage. Take a quick trip around your home and look for wasted space. When we did just that in our small home, we found lots of it. None of the areas under our beds was being used to store anything. We only had three closets, but they had a lot of unused vertical space at the top of them. Just above the clothes-hanging bar was a shelf. But above the shelf was nothing, leaving about three feet of unused space between the shelf and the ceiling. Because we never stacked items three feet high, we had about two feet of space that we could use. Multiply that by the width and depth of those three closet shelves, and we were looking at about 20 cubic feet of storage space.

We had my father build shelves in one of the closets and then purchased some plastic stacking shelves at a yard sale for the others. Then we put in those high places items we needed only occasionally throughout the year, like holiday bulbs and garlands, tax information, seasonal table runners and decorations, and so on.

Also thinking vertically in your basement can help to create space. Any container that stacks well, be it store-bought and plastic or free and cardboard, can help free up space. Learn to stack up, not side by side.

Another great idea that came to us happened one day after church. We needed to stop by the grocery store to grab one simple item. Todd let me off at the front and then circled the store parking lot a few times to keep the baby sleeping in his car seat. As he rounded the back of the building, something caught his eye. It was a large, metal, triple-stacking bin on wheels that was made to hold Twizzlers candy. The store was through with it and ready to dispose of it. We asked the manager if we could have it, and he was more than happy to have us take it off his hands. We were thrilled! You see, we had been looking for a way to store all of the kids' playthings in our tiny one-car garage. This contraption was perfect! It was sturdy, had three vertical bins, and with the wheels on the bottom, it was perfect for rolling in and out of the garage when they wanted to retrieve a ball, glove, jump rope, or Frisbee to play with. It was another way that God provided for a seemingly trivial need as we sought to be a family of hospitality. From then on we obtained many storage items from grocery, department, and drug stores including an awesome large, three-tiered, see-through plastic holder that took up only about four square feet of space. We used it to store our kids' toys in, assigning one tier per child. It stored three times more than our toy box using about the same amount of floor space, and the kids could see through the clear plastic to find just what they were looking for.

Try going into these places of business and speaking to the store manager. Ask him or her if they will call you before they throw out a display case or bin so you can take a look at it first. Most stores are happy to do this for you. Better that their unneeded shelves and bins end up in your house than in a landfill.

How about under beds? As I mentioned, under our beds was nothing except a healthy family of dust bunnies. More unused space! We purchased several under-the-bed boxes during a January storage sale at our local department store. In these we placed off-season clothes and blankets and our camping items, and one entire box housed our wrapping paper, greeting cards, ribbons, and bows.

Need more ideas? Try under stairwells and in the garage, attic, or shed. There have to be nooks and crannies in your home that would make for wonderful storage spaces. If not, think function. Instead of a coffee table, use an antique or new trunk you can store things in. In our first apartment, old orange crates doubled as end tables and book holders. Stackable hat boxes of various sizes can be covered with wallpaper samples and used to store smaller items. Just put on your thinking cap and you'll come up with many ideas.

I never cease to be amazed how God is concerned about the little things in life. Oh yes, he is involved in issues like world hunger, the war on terror, and the other "biggies" of life, but he is also ever present in the small matters. Jeremiah 33:3 says, "Call to me and I will answer you and tell you great and unsearchable things that you do not know." Well, maybe you don't know how you will ever be able to use your place as a means for blessing others through hospitality because it is small. Tell God. He knows your frustration and is ready to show himself strong as he takes each excuse and hurls it into outer space.

Remember, what he calls you to do, he will enable you to do. Keep praying, watching, and brainstorming. He is faithful. And he is willing to use imperfect people residing in ordinary homes as an avenue of spreading his blessing to others.

✎Welcome Ideas✎

Be a Tourist in Your Own Hometown

If you don't have a house large enough to host another fam-
ily comfortably, consider letting local attractions do the hosting.
Invite others to join you as you take in some local area attractions.
Here are some ideas to get you started:

- ❧ Visit a local museum and then go out for coffee and sodas.
- ❧ Take in a local sporting event. Our family has enjoyed the
  minor league baseball franchise in a neighboring town. These
  events are designed to be family friendly. Plan and bring
  along a tailgate dinner consisting of sub sandwiches, chips,
  pop, and cookies, or bring a small portable grill and cook
  brats before the big game.
- ❧ Trek off to a water park or nearby lake. Pack a picnic lunch
  and take along some Frisbees or sand and water toys. This
  idea works especially well with a few moms of young children. The kids can splash in the water while the moms enjoy
  some adult conversation.
- ❧ Invite a new family out for ice cream at an area parlor after
  an evening event at church.
- ❧ Take an expedition to the local zoo along with another family.
  Enjoy dinner at a local burger joint afterward.
- ❧ If you are near a large university, call and ask for a listing
  of their local attractions. Our nearby Michigan State University has beautiful botanical gardens, a butterfly house,
  an on-campus dairy and ice cream store, and an awesome
  planetarium. Take your company to one of these fun hands-
  on places and then back to your home for a simple snack.

- ❧ Check your local paper for outdoor concerts and theatrical productions. Invite someone who would enjoy seeing such shows. Spread a blanket out and take along some sandwiches, fruit, and a thermos of iced tea.

- ❧ Many towns have wonderful nature centers that are perfect for exploring on a sunny afternoon. Host others there for an outing before taking in a light lunch at a local café.

- ❧ Meet a friend who is struggling at a coffee shop. Order two lattes or mochas and a decadent chocolate-covered shortbread or yummy fruit muffin—your treat. After listening to her, ask her for one or two specific ways you can pray for her.

Efficient Entertaining Ideas

When our family of five lived in a small house with an even smaller eat-in kitchen, we learned to be creative when it came to hosting others for food. If you too are in a situation where space is limited, try some innovative get-togethers like these:

If serving an entire hot meal is not an option, try lap meals. Serve up a slow cooker of taco meat with all of the fixings for nachos: lettuce, cheese, tomatoes, salsa, sour cream, and guacamole. Guests can make a plate tailored to their liking. For dessert, offer a variety of ice cream novelties on a stick.

Instead of a meal, invite others over for a simple snack. Make popcorn or homemade caramel corn (recipe on page 62). Serve with a special drink such as root beer floats or hot apple cider. Start collecting thick glass mugs to keep in your freezer. When you pour in the root beer or cider, the mugs frost up just like at a restaurant. Spread a blanket on the floor and play a board game or two.

Try a baked potato bar. Make several large baked potatoes wrapped in foil. Keep warm in a slow cooker set on low. Provide a stovetop and counter of various toppings. Try cheese sauce, steamed broccoli, sautéed mushrooms, taco meat, shredded cheeses, bacon bits, sour cream, butter, salt, pepper, chives, and pizza sauce with chopped pepperoni. Your company can custom make their spuds adding their favorite toppings. Add a simple drink and homemade cookies for dessert. Make a batch or two using your favorite drop cookie recipes. Make them monster sized and add a few minutes to the recipe's baking time.

Utilize the warm summer months or a sunny fall day to entertain your guests with an outdoor meal. Serve traditional picnic fare or grill out some burgers, hot dogs, chicken, or chops. Try some grilling packet ideas. Simply spray large squares of foil with nonstick cooking spray. Then place a piece of meat on and top it with a variety of combos. Try a pork chop topped with a dash of soy sauce, 3 tablespoons of cream of mushroom soup, and a few onion and green pepper slices. Or try a chicken breast with a dash of olive oil and a little lemon juice or some Italian dressing and a slice each of lemon and onion. Seal the foil tightly. Grill over medium heat for 20–30 minutes. Play yard games or take a walk to a local park. Return home to catch fireflies in the summer or have a bonfire complete with s'mores for a sweet ending.

Hold an old-fashioned ice cream social. You provide the ice cream, either store bought or hand cranked. Guests bring various toppings.

How about a meal of leftovers? My friend Kendra often invites several families to bring over their favorite board games and refrigerator leftovers on Sunday evenings. They then have a game night and smorgasbord of edible items from which to choose.

Just inviting others over for dessert is still a way to offer hospitality. These are relatively easy to eat while balancing your plate on your lap. Serve an assortment of pies and cakes—store bought is fine—and coffee, hot cocoa, or flavored teas.

Think seasonal. In the winter serve assorted Christmas cookies and hot cocoa and coffee to drink. In spring or summer, try assorted cut-up fruits, slices of melon, or an assortment of veggies and dill dip. For fall, serve hot spiced cider and fresh donuts. Or try this yummy apple dip: Mix ¾ cup brown sugar, ¼ cup sugar, 1 teaspoon vanilla, and 8 ounces cream cheese. Blend well. Just before serving, add 1 cup chopped salted peanuts. Serve with a tart apple such as Granny Smith or Cortland. To keep apples from turning brown, soak in lemon-lime pop and drain before serving.

Have a salad buffet. Guests can bring various fruit, veggie, or pasta salads. Serve along with fresh-squeezed lemonade. A plate of salads is easy to balance on the lap.

∽ 6 ∾

Decorating on a Shoestring

The time had finally come. We were moving into a new home. It was a bit bigger than the 900-plus square foot one we had called home for the past eleven years. This new ranch style abode was 1200 square feet with about 800 square feet of the basement finished as well. We were thrilled! Although it certainly isn't a huge house by our town's standards, it was only two years old and had been built by a reputable trim carpenter who finished it off beautifully—oak floors, crown molding, and a huge built-in computer center and bookshelf area on the lower level. We could hardly wait to move all of our things into this new place.

Uh oh. Now there was the problem. We didn't quite have enough belongings to furnish this place. You see, we were "movin' on up" from our two-bedroom bungalow to a three-bedroom place with a large extra family room and a school/toy room in the basement, nearly doubling our square footage. And the items we did have were hand-me-downs and garage sale finds.

Also, up until that time, all three of our children shared one bedroom. Poor Mackenzie. She was nearly ten and had never known her own room, except for the first three years of her life when she resided in the little room off of our bedroom that we had made into a nursery. Since then she had bunked with at least one boy, and she currently shared her quarters with two kid brothers. Was her room pink and frilly and feminine like many of her friends' rooms?

Hardly. They shared a triple bunk donned with basic blue blankets. The room was a rather eclectic mix. Sure, there were a few dainty dolls and sweet stuffed animals. But mostly there were Hot Wheels cars on the dresser, Curious George books in the book basket, and Batman underwear in the drawers. What's a girl to do?

Thankfully, our daughter took it all in stride. Although she would have loved to have her own room, we never really dealt with a bad attitude from her. A mother hen type, she enjoyed reading books to the boys at night and playing the part of big sister. But we knew that she would be delighted when someday she could have a room decorated just for her. Now was our chance.

We wanted Kenzie to have a room that was in her taste and matched her personality. She chose lavender walls and a colorful daisy border to match. We had no idea what we were going to do for furniture. Until that time, all three kids shared that metal triple bunk and were using two dressers that were from Todd's childhood bedroom and became ours when we were first married. We decided to use the dressers in the boys' room and sell the bunks at our garage sale.

Often in our life we have made a prayer list of items we feel we need. We learned years ago that before venturing out to buy an item at full price, we should give God the opportunity to provide the item at a great sale price, used for still less, or sometimes even for free. We have seen God answer our prayers over and over again. We document these in our family's "I Spy" book—a simple spiral notebook that chronicles the faith stories of how God blessed us with material possessions that we needed and prayed for.

We even go as far as to make a garage sale prayer list with the specifics listed. Each year by the end of the season, most of the items are crossed off as we find them at sales around our town or in secondhand and thrift shops.

Well, this particular year, our list was a doozy! We needed an entire bedroom suite for Kenzie, beds for the boys, a dining room table and chairs, appliances for the kitchen, and furniture for the lower level family room and schoolroom. Would we ever find it all? Our list was usually much shorter. We noted clothing pieces or small items like roller blades for the kids or a wheelbarrow for gardening. But this time we were talking big-ticket items. And we didn't have a great deal of cash left after buying the house. No major shopping spree here.

We decided to go out on a limb and trust God anyway. In our hearts we knew that he had picked this place out just for us. We even put an offer on it before the house hit the market. We closed on the house in April but weren't moving in until August. God had four months to work. Our kids reminded us that he only needed six days to create the world. Certainly he could furnish our dwelling in four months!

I didn't want "garage sale-ing" to consume my entire summer, so I scoured the classified ads and decided to hit only the ones that sounded promising. Mackenzie and I ventured off one morning to a wealthy suburb. An advertisement had listed "girls' bedroom suite" as one of its items.

We got to the sale a few minutes before it opened and my heart sank. There were already at least twenty cars lining the streets and shoppers waiting in the driveway. We hopped out and took our place at the back of the pack. I decided that if God wanted us to have that bedroom suite, we weren't going to need to be pushy in the process.

A couple of minutes later the garage door rolled open. The room was packed with stuff as well as several items of furniture. I sent Kenzie ducking into the pack to try to make her way to the bedroom suite to grab the price tag off of it and bring it to me. I, in the meantime, was going to try to locate the owner. But how could I pick him or her out in the midst of this crowd? Lord, help!

Again God heard the smallest, seemingly insignificant request from a mom on a mission. I spotted a man out of the corner of my eye eating a bagel and holding a cup of coffee. I'd seen a few ladies in the driveway sporting travel mugs, but no men, and certainly none of them had a bagel. He had to be the homeowner. I'd found him!

Arms were reaching, purses were swaying, and bodies were shoving as the people tried to grab the items they wanted or take tags off of the big pieces.

"Excuse me, sir. How much for your girls' bedroom set?" I inquired.

"I think we put $100 on it. It has five pieces," he replied.

Before he could even take another bite of that bagel, I blurted out, "I'll take it!"

"All right," he said, "but you'll need to bring me the tag in case someone else has already spoken for it."

At that I turned around and Kenzie suddenly appeared right behind me. With a huge grin on her face, she handed me the tag and longingly asked, "Can we buy it, Mommy?"

"Done!" I exclaimed as I took the tag from her and handed it to the man. He smiled when he realized our divide and conquer plan had worked.

We continued looking for other trinkets and treasures as I walked over to examine the furniture set. I nearly cried. You see, we couldn't afford to be really picky. This was for a nine-year-old girl, after all. It needn't be anything fancy. If it was functional, it would do. But upon closer examination, I could hardly believe my eyes.

It was an older but well built and beautiful ivory-colored French Provincial set from a well-to-do furniture store in that town. There was scarcely a nick or scratch on it, even though the gentleman later told me they had bought it for their daughter when she was six or seven and she had just finished college. It had a large dresser, a mirror, a nightstand, a desk, and a bookshelf to boot! It had been maintained meticulously and looked nearly new.

For fun, when we got home, I looked up what a similar set would cost at that store new. This one probably would have cost close to $2,000. The owner could have easily sold that set ten times over. The other shoppers who were interested in it didn't know what had hit them!

Kenzie's faith was stretched that day. I did assure her that God was not some genie in a bottle ready to grant our every wish, but he does reward those who are faithful and provides for our every need. Perhaps this was his way of blessing a little girl who had been so willing to wait and in the meantime had made her shared quarters with her boy brothers a happy and welcoming place. (We did have to chuckle once we moved into our new house and the kids had separate rooms for the first time. They didn't want to be apart! The boys spent the first few months camped out on their sister's floor. That way they could still have her read them a bedtime story and sing the "Goodnight Boys" song from our summer church camp before they drifted off to sleep!)

Our daughter's bedroom set was only the beginning of the journey of blessing that God was taking us on. That summer we also found a beautiful solid oak kitchen table with leaves enough to make seating space for ten. We found a set of five chairs to match that were from a very reputable furniture store. We had been hoping to find six chairs, but these were of such fine quality for a fraction of the original cost that we snatched them up. Besides, we had five people in our family, so it would work for us.

A few weeks after purchasing those chairs, we found ourselves shopping in the nearby small town where the well-known, family-owned furniture store our chairs came from was located. I knew that the chairs were over ten years old, though they looked brand new. I was pretty certain that the store didn't sell that style anymore. But I reasoned that if they did, we'd bought the set of five for so little that we could afford to pay full price for one more to round out our set.

We went in and looked around in the dining room section. Although we could find some pieces similar to the chairs we had obtained, they weren't exact matches. Then as I was describing the chair to a salesman, another worker came over and said he thought that he had just such a chair up in his office. He went upstairs and returned a few moments later carrying the long-lost match to our set of chairs! The store sold it to us at a great price, and we had a complete set for our new home.

We found many other items over the course of the summer, including a big side-by-side refrigerator and a trundle bed set for our boys. When the time came for us to move in, we had all the rooms perfectly furnished with nice pieces that matched and fit. Our "I Spy" notebook began to burst at the seams as we recorded our Creator's faithfulness. At the end of the summer we added up what all of those appliances and furnishings would have cost us if we had purchased them new and at full price, and the grand total was nearly $10,000. But God saw to it that we only had to fork out a little over $1,500. Isn't he amazing?

We were blown away as we thought about how real he became to us and our kids that summer. Our children experienced answered prayer. They joined us as we believed and then watched

God provide. Our family was drawn together in a special way as we anticipated using our new home as a center of God's love and care for those in our life.

It can be the same for you and your family. If you long to use your home as a center of welcome but fear you don't have enough living area, seating space, or eating room, tell him! Ask for creativity. Inquire about opportunities. Beg for ideas. Look through the eyes of faith to envision your home as a center equipped for offering "house-pitality" to others. Expect God to answer in ways far beyond what you could ever imagine. Remember, God will supply all of your needs . . . but apparently not all your wants. Our garage sale list is still on our fridge. "Jacuzzi" has not been crossed off!

Getting the Look

I think most of us desire for our surroundings to be pleasant, but we don't always feel we possess the money or know-how to make it that way. What part does having a tastefully decorated home play in extending welcome to others? Do we need to have beautifully adorned places in order to offer hospitality? Is there a way to do this without blowing our budgets?

Oh, yes. I believe wholeheartedly that God delights in our desire to provide a pleasant atmosphere for our family and others who will grace our home, as long as we keep proper perspective. We should want to make their time with us welcoming and inviting and to make available to them refreshment—and I'm not just talking about the food! Our homes can by their very décor, atmosphere, and surroundings help others to forget the cares of the outside world and be refreshed by the love of the Lord. Our surroundings can help us to accomplish that very goal.

Am I talking about hiring an interior designer to make your place look like it hopped off the pages of the latest magazine?

No, although there is certainly nothing wrong with doing that if you can afford to. But most of you reading this book probably have somewhat limited money and resources. How can you make your place pleasing without breaking the bank?

First of all, let's make sure we know what we are aiming for. In the survey I conducted with women of all ages and stages, I asked them just how important it was to them that someone's home be decorated in a fancy or expensive manner. That response received a 3.1. However, that the home be tastefully decorated in an inviting manner received an 8.3. Just what does that mean?

The definition of *tasteful* includes words like harmonious, graceful, sensitive, and aesthetic. It in no way has anything to do with being costly, luxurious, or expensive. Rather, it is an atmosphere of simple beauty, of calm rest.

Have you ever been in a home like this? Maybe it hasn't been the nicest or fanciest home you've ever been in, but it is one whose very walls beckon you to come and "sit a spell." My spiritual mother Pat's home was just such a place, and remember, it hadn't been redecorated in over a decade! So what was it that drew me to it time and time again?

Many things. First, it was clean and clutter free, with enough space to sit and visit. It was steeped in love, with the smell of something good to eat lingering in the air and the sound of praise music wafting in the background. I loved being there, and once gone, I couldn't wait to return. Just being with Pat in her home helped to refresh and reenergize me. I was a new bride trying to build a godly marriage without having had many real role models. As I tried and often failed as a new wife, spending time with Pat at her house helped to get me back on the right road again. She was a breath of fresh air, and her home served as my refueling center. Once I entered, I had time to calm down and share my hurts and hopes with her. She would speak truth to me from God's Word and her years of experience as a pastor's wife.

A Life That Says Welcome

Her words of wisdom often helped to smooth the rough roads and renewed my vision for my life as a youth pastor's wife. Pat's décor matched her personality. All around were signs of God. Her Bible often lay open where she had just finished reading it. Scriptures adorned the walls. Comfy blankets were nearby, ready to be snuggled in while sipping a cup of hot tea or cocoa. Although her colors weren't up-to-date or her furniture of the latest style, her home was welcoming. And yours can be too.

So where to start? First, take an inventory of your home. How does it rate on the clutter scale? It is hard to visit when papers, laundry, and toys are in our way or underfoot. If your living room has no space to sit and visit, consider dejunking and reorganizing as outlined in chapter 4.

If you can, try to have one room that stays relatively clutter free as a rule. No toys and trinkets, no clean or dirty laundry, no junk mail or magazines. A room that invites you to sit down and unwind.

This was not always easy for us. In our first two apartments as well as the first home we owned, space was at a minimum. But we found ways, even in our barely 400-square-foot apartment, to make sure our living room stayed picked up. Here are a small number of things we did.

Even before we had children, we made toys a part of our home. An antique crate in the corner held a few toys, dolls, and trucks for the children of our friends to play with when they visited. This way they weren't strewn about or left out all over the house. They were nearby, ready to be played with, but had a "home" where they belonged when no longer in use.

Even if there are no children residing in your quarters, consider doing the same thing for those whom you will entertain. Many moms have shared with me that they would love to visit others to offer encouragement or drop by someone's home occasionally, but they feel that because they often have a few children in tow, it is rather difficult. If there is nothing for their children to do while there or the house is full of breakables, they may opt out of visiting at all. Make the little people in your life feel welcomed. All it takes are a few toys, a coloring book and crayons, a couple of storybooks, or a child-friendly DVD. You can better minister to a mom when her child is happily busy in your home.

Also, we tried to keep our living room area from becoming the family "catch-all" for laundry, junk mail, and other clutter. Yes, you may need to use your living room to fold laundry. We did for many years before having a basement family room. What you need is to find a system that works and then work the system! Also, don't let those oft-repeated words that are sure to destroy your sense of living room calm creep into your vocabulary. Those words are "For now." You know, "I'll set this basket of unfolded laundry here *for now*." "Just put that junk mail on the coffee table *for now*." Pretty soon our living area is overflowing with piles of "for now" staring us in the face and making us feel defeated!

I encourage baskets and bins. These can be purchased relatively inexpensively at department stores or online, or you can locate some at yard sales and thrift shops. Have one for your magazines, another for unread mail, still another for newspapers. Somehow having all the like items together in a pretty basket takes away the look of clutter. However, don't just leave them there to pile up. Periodically weed through them and deal with your paper and "stuff" or you'll only be prolonging the inevitable—creeping clutter!

Once your clutter is behaving and at bay, you can focus on the décor itself—the walls, window treatments, furniture, rugs, and wall décor. While there is no slick, one-size-fits-all solution to your decorating woes, there are some questions you can ask yourself to try to find your unique style.

For starters, what are your "nonnegotiables"? These would be aspects of your home that you simply cannot change. Do you have small living spaces, off-color carpet, or a certain type of wood trim that you cannot alter? Well then, that is where you will have to begin. Rather than letting it hem you in, make it work for you! I have seen women take an unattractive color of carpet that was not worn enough to replace and with a little ingenuity make it part of a stunning living space. If it is a color you don't particularly care for, try to think of other colors you are fond of that will complement it. One room I saw had carpet in a shade of peach that wasn't particularly attractive, but once the colors of terra cotta, warm nutmeg, and neutral sand were added, it was gorgeous!

Small spaces also cause concern. Try to think out of the box when arranging furniture. Don't simply use the old "couch and chairs face the usual focal point of the television" routine. Try angling your furniture in a corner. Bring a couch away from a wall to make a smaller space open up. Arrange furniture in an L pattern so that some pieces only have an end of them bordering a wall. Get rid of the TV altogether by moving it into a spare bedroom turned den or another part of the house.

Next, decide what pieces you especially can't afford to replace at the moment. (And in the meantime, start a decorating fund for future purchases.) Maybe you have a couch, a chair, or an entire set you are simply going to have to make work. Think what you could do to spruce it up. Invest in a fresh cover? How about some new throw pillows or a small decorative blanket? I have seen old pieces of furniture undergo serious transformations with only modestly priced slipcovers. Those in khaki or denim are washable, durable, and wonderfully neutral. The decorating possibilities with these fabrics are endless!

Before going too far, you must decide if the walls need a sprucing up with paint or can remain their current shade. If going with a new color, keep in mind the following: flat paint is less expensive, reflects less light in the evening, yet shows the most dirt and wear. It can, however, be touched up easily without leaving paint marks. Eggshell or satin finishes reflect a little light and clean up easier than flat. Semigloss and high gloss are the most washable yet really shine with light reflection at night. These are usually reserved for high-traffic, frequently scrubbed rooms such as kitchens and bathrooms. If you like the look of flat paint but want your walls to be scrubbable, I highly recommend flat ceramic paint. My friend Carmen, a painting expert, turned us on to this. She helped us to paint our living room a soothing shade of sage green. It often gets touched by sticky fingers and dirty palms yet cleans up as new. Despite the high volume of kid traffic at our house, we have yet to use paint to touch it up.

Try to put in place a plan for the look you are aiming for. Do you like sleek and contemporary? How about rustic and primitive? Maybe you enjoy frilly and Victorian? As you obtain pieces to round out your décor, keep in mind the style you want. Also, try moving items and wall hangings from one room to another. My friend Andie used to have a décor consulting business. She would go into a home and teach the owner how to rearrange their furniture and other belongings in a new, never-before-thought-of manner. She moved pieces from room to room and wall to wall. Often she could achieve a totally new look using whatever raw materials the homeowner already had. Consider trying the same thing in your home. If you don't feel you have an eye for such tasks, enlist the help of a friend who does.

If you can, try to bring your faith into your décor. Beautiful wall and desk crosses, paintings with Scripture verses on them, and much more are readily available today. Watch for store sales or check online auctions such as eBay to find these. If money is really tight, simply find a picture or painting you love and matte it using a light color. Then, by means of a calligraphy pen if you dare, pen a verse of Scripture on it. Again, if you are not so confident in your ability to do this, find a friend who is. Having our faith visible in our surroundings not only serves as a witness to others but can serve as a reminder to us as well. Choose verses of special significance to you and your family.

My friend Trish Smith began a home business selling beautiful wooden Scripture signs done in an antiqued, crackle painted manner. I have three hanging in our home, keeing God's Word ever before our eyes. For more information and a price list, email her at homespunhearts3@yahoo.com. If you have a favorite Scripture or saying, she takes custom orders too!

While you may not be able to do a major overhaul on every room in your home, pick one or two. Then keep going as time and money allow. Don't aim for fancy but for sweet and simple. Keep the lines clean, the clutter gone or at least disguised, and remember, less is more. The less you have causing clutter or confusion on your walls and floors, the more inviting your abode will be.

And keep this admonition in the forefront of your mind: the most inviting aspect of your home will be your attitude as others dwell within. Serve them. Pamper them. Listen to them, and make every effort to point them to the Lord. Keep in mind that you may not be able to make your home a showcase of beauty and glamour, but you can make it a haven of rest and retreat from an outside world that is often harsh and cruel. Others can think of your home, even with your limited resources, as I did my friend Pat's—as one of their favorite places to be.

↩Welcome Ideas↪

Decorating Basics

Now, I don't want to sound like I am talking out of both sides of my mouth. Your physical surroundings really are not the most important aspect of hospitality. Attitude and love override carpet and commodities. And again, it all comes down to your motives—are you trying to impress or to create an atmosphere of warmth so others can relax and unwind at your house? If the latter is your goal, here are some of the experts' tips that can help you acquire an inviting place.

Mood—What is the look you are going for? Do you want the room to be calm and relaxing, or lively and fun? What activities will primarily take place in this room? Is it a room to sit and read in? Is it a lively family room where you will play board games and snack? Is it a restful master or guest bedroom, or one for a whimsical teen or bouncing boy? Decide what you want the room to say. Then decorate around it.

Color—This is where you can start to achieve the look you are shooting for. Warm colors such as taupes, terra cotta, and mustard gold add warmth. Colors in the cool family like blues, plums, or blue-greens tend to soften a room. Dark colors make a room appear smaller; light colors open rooms up and make them seem larger. If you are afraid to try bold colors on your walls, opt instead for a neutral shade such as oatmeal, light beige, or antique white. Most decorating experts say if you are just starting out, keep it neutral. You can always add splashes of color in your curtains, pillows, or bed coverings. Almost all the experts agree that one color should be somewhere in your house, preferably in your kitchen or main bathroom: yellow. It adds cheer and creates a welcoming feeling.

Texture—Varying the textures in a room creates depth and character. Mix flat, shiny cottons; nubby, hearty plaids; ribbed corduroys; and multi-textured solids and patterns.

Collections—Feel free to display your collections, as long as they don't end up looking like an aisle of clutter at a flea market. Try to keep continuity in your collections. If you are collecting cookie jars, keep the colors, although different, of the same intensity—perhaps mild, muted tones or bright, primary colors.

Function—Try to blend style and function: an antique trunk to hide your warm throws; some large hat boxes painted in shades to complement your room to serve as storage space for smaller items. Or keep your newspapers and magazines in an old Radio Flyer wagon turned coffee table.

Change—One aspect of living in Michigan that I love is that we get to enjoy the changing seasons. Lush, green springtime; the bright sun and shimmering sand of summer; fall foliage in golds, oranges, reds, and browns; and the sparkling white snow and deep blue (and sometimes gray) skies of winter. If God is seasonal, we should be too. With a little ingenuity, you can afford to change your home's look slightly each season. Check end-of-season sales, markdown bins, and clearance aisles for curtains, comforters, table runners, and other décor. My friend Karen has a cute built-in shelf in her circa 1920s kitchen. She changes the décor on this shelf with the changing seasons—snowmen in winter, bunnies and such in spring. I always enjoy seeing what she has displayed when I visit.

Book It!

My friend Carmen is one of the most creative gals I know when it comes to decorating a home. She has an eye for color. How else can I explain the fact that she talked me, Miss Nice and Neutral, into painting my cathedral-high living room walls a bold shade of "gum leaf" green? When she showed me the swatch, I wasn't quite sure I could make the leap. But Carmen has tried many daring hues on her own walls, always with great success. She also has a way with so many other components of decorating: seasonal centerpieces, creative displays of photographs, painting techniques, nontraditional candleholders, and the list just goes on.

I asked her one day how she ever came to be so skilled at styling her home. "Let me show you," she said as she took an old-style photo album off her shelf—the kind with pieces of clear film to be peeled back in order to place the photographs on the page. Carmen had used this album to collect magazine clippings of decorating and centerpiece ideas, painting techniques, and must-try recipes. She had them arranged by category for ease in locating. If she saw anything that struck her fancy or an idea she thought might be fun to try out when hosting a party, into the album it went.

You see, Carmen has never taken a formal class in decorating. She doesn't hold a degree in design. She has gotten her education the old-fashioned way, by observing, studying, and making a point to remember what she has seen. Most of these magazines she obtains from her mother or others who are getting ready to toss them. You can do the same. Doctor's offices, hospital waiting rooms, and public libraries get rid of their magazines on a regular basis. Check with them to see if they have any titles you would be interested in taking from them. Many garage sales have boxes of magazines for a dime a piece or less. Thumb through a few to see if they can inspire you in your quest to spruce your place up a bit.

Decorating with Style

As a mom with young children I would often be frustrated looking at decorating magazines because the rooms in my home never resembled the rooms in those beautiful, glossy pictures. However, my attitude changed as one day I read the following (roughly paraphrased) in one of my favorite magazines: "The bedroom displays a striking combination of stripes, plaids, and florals, all unified by a common color palette." To me it just looked like someone couldn't decide what fabric they liked best and so had used them all. And that's when it hit me—the secret to true decorating with style: it's not *how* you decorate; it's how you *describe* your decorating. In a flash my mind began to imagine how my home would be written up in one of those magazines: "While the living room shows a more traditional side of the homeowner, the Darth Vader mask and green light saber on the coffee table lend an air of surprise and whimsy. The kitchen is reminiscent of a modern art gallery, with the refrigerator and walls displaying original artwork in a variety of media, including paint, markers, craft sticks, and glitter. The basement is liberally sprinkled with action figures while the blanket fort lends a rustic feel to the area. In the back entryway the homeowners cleverly bring the outdoors in by creatively displaying sand, grass clippings, and whatever the cat has caught the night before." As my fantasy tour ended, I realized that my home was decorated exactly as it should be when one has children. And to be honest, I wouldn't trade any of my original artwork for a priceless masterpiece. So remember the secret to decorating with style: decorating is in the eye (and the description) of the beholder.

Contributed by Karen Leif

Decorate on a Shoestring

Give a room a new look with quick ideas that add charm:

- Make curtain tiebacks from anything interesting: boat rope for a nautical theme, traditional plaid or brightly striped ribbon, various widths and styles of chains, braided strips of leftover fabric, or ready-made lengths of ruffle.

꙾ Inventive window valances can be made with fish netting, several coordinating square cloth napkins hung over the rod with the corners pointing down, or pretty twin sheets draped over the rod or tied in knots in the middle or at the corners.

꙾ For custom-made window shades, purchase inexpensive shades at the department store, then cut fabric to coordinate with your bedspread and glue on with spray adhesive.

꙾ Fashion headboards out of anything unusual: a portion of picket fence painted white, an old bookcase, a discarded fireplace mantle.

꙾ Create a family heritage wall. Purchase antique-looking or inexpensive black frames from a dollar store. Select copies (not the originals) of black-and-white or old colored photos of your family from generations past. Paint the wall you'll use with a light cream-colored semigloss paint. When that is dry, paint a coat of warm oatmeal-colored paint to which clear glaze has been added. (Glazes are available at most department stores—follow directions on side of can.) Using an inexpensive wallpaper brush, make a textured pattern to resemble old linen by wiping the brush side to side and then up and down. Frame some copies of old letters to hang alongside the framed photos. In front of it all place a small table with an old leather Bible, antique reading glasses, and a hurricane lamp or antique-looking candlestick.

꙾ Wield a wedding wall. In an open stairwell or another prominent location, hang various-sized framed pictures of your loved ones from their weddings. Include both black-and-white and colored pictures of both young and old. On our wedding wall we included a shelf with a bar for displaying a hanging quilt, and on the shelf we placed a potted dried hydrangea and a set of candlesticks along with a few more pictures. This wall serves as a visual reminder to pray for these couples and their marriages.

❧ Add personality to a room by stenciling a wall. Keep the design simple by just going around the top and a few inches down the sides of window or door frames with an ivy stencil. Or scatter a few hearts, butterflies, or baseballs and footballs above a bed or dressers. Premade craft sponge shapes work well for this.

❧ Give a room a faux finish. Experiment with techniques on a piece of poster board first before doing it on the wall. Try different items: a rolled-up rag, feather duster tips dipped in paint, a wadded-up plastic grocery sack, sponges, or a wallpaper brush. Don't limit yourself to walls. Faux paint terra cotta pots, hat boxes, old wooden bowls, or wooden dressers or desks purchased at yard sales. Don't pick highly contrasting colors as the result will look blotchy. Choose colors that are two or three shades apart on the color strip swatches at the store. The result will appear more marbled or have more of a wallpaper look. For best results, use a satin or semigloss finish. My favorite is cream on an oatmeal color. It's neutral enough that you can still change the look of the room often (or seasonally) by changing window valances, comforters, and other fabric items in the room like pillows or slipcovers. Remember, dark colors make a room appear smaller, and light colors typically open up a room.

❧ To add depth to your paint job, mix your own sand paint. Mix 1 pint of fine grain silica sand into a half gallon of latex flat paint. Paint onto prepared wall (either over flat paint or, if a gloss paint is on the wall, sand and paint wall with a coat of primer first). Try doing the bottom half of the room a different color than the top half. Place a border or chair rail in between, approximately 36 inches from the floor.

❧ Hang pictures with nails but create the illusion that they are hung with ribbon by making a bow with satin ribbon and then attaching it several inches above the frame and running two strips of the ribbon down to the top corners of the picture.

❧ Spray hairspray onto dried flowers to keep them from shedding. Place in an array of baskets or crocks purchased from garage sales and secondhand stores.

Sensational Centerpieces

❧ Place several candles of the same color but differing sizes and heights on a round or oval mirror as a beautiful centerpiece, especially for holidays. The mirror gently reflects the flames, giving off a warm glow.

❧ For a pretty spring centerpiece display, slice in half various citrus fruits—oranges, grapefruits, lemons, limes. Lay the pieces cut side up and carve a hole large enough for a votive candle in them. Arrange them into a rectangle or oval on some sunny-colored fabric cut with pinking shears.

❧ Sugar, salt, or sand can make up the base of your centerpiece. Place it on a cookie sheet with sides. The salt or sugar look like snow for a winter theme—add small snowmen, little pine trees, etc. The sand is great for a summer piece with seashells and sand toys sprinkled about.

❧ For a family birthday, scatter pictures of the birthday boy or girl on the table. Cover with a clear plastic tablecloth.

❧ Combine items from nature with candles to create instant ambience and set a welcoming mood:

⊙ Using an apple corer, cut a hole 1 ½ inches deep into several shapes and colors of apples. Work a candle into each hole. Display on your kitchen table on a runner made

A Life That Says Welcome

of fall-colored plaid fabric. Mini-pumpkins and gourds also can be hollowed out to make candleholders or small vases.

⊚ Place a fresh artichoke in a small terra cotta pot. Cut a hole in the center large enough to hold a small pillar candle.

⊚ Place bay leaves side by side around the exterior of several small votive candle cups. These are a dime a dozen at yard sales. Use Scotch tape to secure leaves in place. Tie with gold or silver ribbon.

⊚ For a centerpiece as fragrant as it is beautiful, fill a medium-sized glass bowl with fresh cranberries. Add water to about three inches in depth. Arrange in the berries some fresh ivory and burgundy-colored roses along with holiday greens like holly, ivy, or evergreen. Place additional small fruits (crab apples, fresh cherries) within the greenery. Place several ivory candles of varying heights around the outside of the bowl. Pretty!

⊚ Make an ice luminary. Center a 2-inch-diameter candle into a clean half gallon cardboard (not plastic) milk carton. Stuff holly around the edges, using it to center and hold the candle. Fill the carton with water, making sure the wick is well above the edge of the carton. Freeze solid. To remove paper, dip in warm water for a few seconds and peel away. Keep luminary frozen till ready to use. Place in shallow glass bowl or tray and cluster more holly around the base. Light the candle and prepare for a beautiful meltdown as your evening progresses. You can also make an ice luminary with slices of fresh citrus fruit for a different look.

❧ Return to our colonial roots by displaying "sugared" fresh fruit around your holiday ham or turkey or piled in a pretty clear bowl. Brush fresh fruit (lemons, oranges, red or green grapes, plums, peaches, or cherries work well) with a light coat of beaten egg white. Roll in sugar for a fresh dusted snow effect. Arrange among fresh greenery, and remind the youngsters (and those young at heart too), "DO NOT EAT!"

❧ Pile a rustic wooden bowl full of seasonal nature items like pinecones, fall leaves, unusual nuts and berries, twigs, and interestingly shaped or colored rocks. A basket of gourds and mini-pumpkins is also nice. For spring, line a bowl with a plaid pastel square of material and pile with fresh fruit and some wrapped candy fruit slices.

❧ Add a touch to the table with napkin rings made from things you already have at home. At the holidays, old tin cookie cutters shaped like bells, stars, and Christmas trees work well coupled with holiday plaid napkins.

❧ If you'd like, incorporate antiques into your décor not only for beauty but for function. My mother-in-law uses an old wooden wagon as a coffee table. It doubles as a storage place for her magazines.

❧ My friend Lisa Connolly suggests picking up an old pair of white ice skates. Replace the shoelaces with cheery red ribbon. Use as a festive centerpiece or an outdoor decoration next to a wooden sled.

❧ A garland of seasonal goodies like dried apple and orange slices, bay leaves, nuts, and cranberries can nicely adorn a hearth or be strung across the top of a window. You may need to drill holes through the nuts for stringing them on the garland.

❧ Or try a whimsical string of gingerbread men. Combine 2 cups of cinnamon (purchased in bulk) with 1 tablespoon of white glue and just enough applesauce, added a spoonful at a time, to make a thick dough. Dust counter and rolling pin with cinnamon and roll out dough. Cut out shapes and lay to dry in cookie sheet dusted with more cinnamon. When dried, hot glue raisins and red hot candies for eyes and buttons. Glue onto twine or red ribbon. Hang and enjoy!

A Life That Says Welcome

∞ 7 ∞

Sure, Stay for Supper!

I awoke that morning with a mind full of mixed emotions. I was excited but apprehensive; eager yet a bit fearful as I contemplated the day ahead. I thought back over my first month of marriage. I had passed some major hurdles, met some important milestones. I had risen to the challenge in the area I was most fearful of as a new bride. Was it keeping house? Meeting my husband's emotional needs? Juggling substitute teaching, a junior varsity coaching assignment, our first home, and a new marriage? No. It was much more terrifying than these. It was the duty I felt I was least qualified to do.

It was cooking for my hubby.

But I had come so far in four weeks! I had started with home-made vegetarian spaghetti sauce over angel hair pasta, the first meal I ever fixed for my beloved. (I was so proud and shocked when it turned out well. We even took a picture of it!) From there I graduated to meatloaf and baked potatoes, lasagna and tossed salad. Then came my specialty: homemade whole wheat pizza. We had that uncomplicated favorite every Thursday night on my husband's day off. We dined on it by candlelight while we watched the one television show we were able to squeeze into our busy schedule, *The Cosby Show*. Soon I was making the crust without looking at the recipe book. Oh yeah, now I was cookin'!

But today was different. Today my skills would be put to the test, for that night I was not just to prepare a meal for my dear partner in life. Oh, no. This was much bigger than that. That night we were having our first ever company for dinner—my husband's boss (our pastor) and his lovely wife.

I was a wreck.

I chose a new meal I hadn't tried out yet in my month-long cooking career. Trust me, gals. That is a big mistake! Never, ever, *ever* serve a new meal to company. I have tried this many times with only about a 50 percent success rate. The other 50 percent? Plain awful. Sometimes inedible! But that night I so wanted to serve something gourmet-sounding and trendy. Something my mother-in-law or one of my gourmet sisters-in-law would make. I couldn't envision them serving up meatloaf or dishing out a plain pasta affair. No, their main dish would have flair, their side dishes would be delish, and certainly their dessert would be something to write home about. Why, by golly, I reckoned mine would be too!

I found a recipe in a magazine for Lemon Herbed Chicken. It sounded straightforward enough. Pieces of skinless chicken in a 9-by-13-inch pan drizzled with olive oil and lemon juice and sprinkled with Italian herbs—basil, oregano, rosemary, and thyme. To top it off, the recipe called for slices of lemons and Vidalia onions to be layered on top. (And yes, I had to ask the grocer just what a Vidalia onion was.) This entree sounded delicious and relatively easy.

Oh, please. Remember my banana cream pie? I could take any recipe that sounded easy and turn it into a culinary catastrophe.

For a side dish I chose large redskin baked potatoes. Easy enough, I surmised, but still restaurant-style quality. Real butter and sour cream were on hand to top them off, along with fresh ground pepper and coarse ground sea salt. You see, my in-laws introduced me to those. Morton and McCormick's just didn't seem gourmet enough anymore.

I picked up some wonderful sweet corn from a local farm market. I was also planning to make crescent rolls. (Okay, not make them but whack 'em open and bake them.) For dessert I made a fresh peach-blueberry pie. From scratch! No fold-out refrigerated crusts here. Yep, it took me all afternoon.

I had to actually sit down and figure out when I would start each component of the meal in order to have them done at the same time. The pie came first, of course. Then the potatoes took an hour and a half at 350 degrees. The chicken recipe called for a 375 degree oven for an hour and fifteen minutes. Hey, how was I going to manage that? I didn't have two ovens! The crescent rolls needed to bake 13 minutes at 375 degrees. The corn needed to boil for ten minutes.

I actually made a flow chart for myself to ensure all was ready at the same time. I figured out that cooking the baked potatoes for fifteen minutes less at a little higher temperature was going to be fine. I set my timer and followed my schedule, taking short breaks to straighten, dust, and sweep as well as touch up my lipstick a bit. Then the apartment buzzer rang. Company was here!

I settled Pastor Fox and his wife into the living area, where my husband engaged in some small talk with them. After a few minutes I announced that dinner was served. They took their seats at our hand-me-down Duncan Phyfe table and chairs. The table was set with our new dishes, the candles were lit, and the food was on, all except the chicken. I just needed to pull that out of the oven.

When I did, I gasped. The chicken looked nothing like the picture in the magazine. Instead, it looked more like dried, burnt rubber with charcoal-crusted squiggles and circles on top. (Those were supposed to be the golden yellow lemons and perfectly caramelized onions.) I couldn't figure out what had happened.

I quickly poured on a little more lemon juice and olive oil, hoping to moisten it up a bit. Then I could only place it on the table and hope it tasted better than it looked.

It didn't.

Thankfully, Mrs. Fox was a gracious guest. She helped me to go over what might possibly have happened. I learned that when cooking on two different racks, the top rack gets the hottest since heat rises. The chicken had been on the top rack. But that wasn't the main culprit. The main culprit was one teeny, tiny word I had somehow overlooked: *covered*.

Oops! I had baked the daylights out of that beautiful bird because the pan wasn't covered in foil like the recipe had plainly instructed. Thankfully, the rest of the meal had turned out okay, and I had prepared plenty to go around. We were able to have an extra potato or ear of corn to fill our chicken-deprived stomachs. The one redeeming part of that meal was a bit of comic relief. Our pastor entered into a long dissertation about some theological issue, using his hands emphatically as he talked, all the while a kernel of butter-soaked corn slid slowly down his cheek and under his jaw. Todd and I tried to keep from bursting into laughter. Finally Mrs. Fox took notice and declared, "Honey, you have a little hitchhiker on your chin."

Besides that moment of humorous reprieve, my first company meal was an obvious flop. I recount the story of it not to garner pity from you. Please don't call Emeril and beg him to give me free food preparation lessons or send me a subscription to a cooking magazine. I'm doing just fine now, thank you very much. I tell you all of this to let you know that if *I* can learn to cook, anyone can! In fact, several of my recipes have brought me "Best of Show" rosettes in our local county fair. (Hmph! Take that, Miss Crocker!) We all have to have a starting point, and if you, like me, have a starting point near zero, you have nowhere else to go but up!

In a relatively short time I was cooking for a crowd with confidence. How did I learn to do it? The same way we learn any aspect of this hospitality routine: practice, practice, practice. The rest of this chapter will be chock-full of little secrets I have learned on the way, recipe ideas, and cooking tips to help you get started.

First and foremost, let's just get rid of any notion that your food needs to be fancy and gourmet. Back to the grass roots. The gals in my survey responded that when it comes to feeling refreshed and welcomed at someone's home, gourmet-type food only scored a 1.7 on the hospitality scale. Having simple, tasty food and plenty of it, on the other hand, received a rating of 9.1. Many women stressed that they felt uncomfortable if they had a large family or a few hungry teenage boys and a small casserole was placed on the table to feed so many mouths. Better to err on the side of too much. You can always utilize the leftovers for a few lunches that week.

Now, as you are going along, once you find a recipe that works wonderfully, a dish that is delicious, or an appetizer that is sure to please, *write it down*! This may seem elementary, but I know that if I use a recipe and add a few twists—less of this, more of that, a dash of something not called for—and then don't write down what I did, it is nearly impossible to repeat the same dish.

Once you find several main dishes, vegetables, sides, and desserts you and your kin take pleasure in, begin to group them into menu plans. Grab some large index cards or a notebook. Decide which main dish goes with what sides and what sweet fare can round out the whole menu. From there, make a list of needed ingredients and their quantities. Then when company is expected, simply choose one of your preplanned menus to serve. This is so much easier than beginning from scratch. And if the dishes are tried-and-true hits with your family, company is sure to delight in them too.

Before planning and cooking for guests, be sure to find out if there are any special needs. Does anyone have allergies or sensitivities to specific foods? Are their children overly picky eaters? While we normally do not allow our own children to be picky, we do try to accommodate guests. At the very least I try to leave certain "yucky" foods—mostly onions, green peppers, and mushrooms—in larger chunks so that they can be easily picked out. I let the children (or finicky adults!) know that it is just fine with me if they do so. Or I practice what my friend and fellow author Nancy Slagle of "30 Day Gourmet" freezer cooking fame preaches. It is a little concept she calls "health by stealth." She simply cooks and purees any veggie deemed "yucky" by her kids—onions, carrots, red and green peppers, and mushrooms, to name a few. Then she adds them to her sauces. Red, orange, and green vegetables hide easily in tomato-based sauces. Mushrooms and onions slip in undetected in white and brown gravies. Ta-da! Health by stealth! When your kiddos ask, "Are there onions in this?" you can boldly retort, "Do you *see* any onions?"

Try to keep in mind the time of day when you plan. Will it be mid-afternoon when a light salad-based menu will work? Will it be an unusually late dinner and the brood will be rather ravenous? What about the time of year? Will it be chilly outside? Opt for a hearty and warm "comfort foods" meal. Will it be so scorching hot outside that a steamy main dish will seem inappropriate? Opt for a crisp vegetable or cool pasta-based entree instead. Will you want to have a theme or ethnic dimension to the meal? Try out several of these dishes too until they become a regular part of your repertoire. You will gain confidence each time you meet with triumph. Remember, practice, practice, practice!

What about keeping on top of your regular planning, shopping, and cooking so that having company every so often doesn't throw you for a loop? A few ideas have worked well for me.

First and foremost, keep a pre-printed grocery list on your refrigerator at all times. You can make one on your computer or even in your sweet little ol' handwriting. List what items you commonly buy for your family and stock your pantry with. Then arrange them in the same order that you will find them in the grocery store, leaving some blank space at the end of each section. Most stores have similar layouts: produce is first, followed by bakery and breads, canned and boxed dry goods, frozen and refrigerated fare. Train the members of your family who are old enough to read to help you keep this list up-to-date. When they use the last squirt of mustard, they circle the word *mustard* on the list. Pour yourself the final bowl of cornflakes? Grab a pen and circle!

When readying yourself to hit the grocer's aisles, this pre printed list will have you already halfway home. Simply add any ingredients in the blank spaces for new dishes you will try that are not part of your regular inventory. If you hit more than one supermarket, accentuate the items that you will get at one store with a brightly colored highlighter. This way you can buy your meats and other ingredients where they are at the best price. Simply consult the store's circular before heading off on your shopping excursion.

If you like to post your menu on your fridge or write it down in your planner, when you eat a meal, cross it off, but circle any items you did not use. For example, let's say you planned a meal with steamed broccoli as a side, but you never got around to making it. Well, rather than letting it go bad, circle the word *broccoli* on your menu to remind you that you need to make soup out of that bunch or cut it up and serve it with dip for an afternoon snack. A great resource for using up these leftover and unused items is *The Use It Up Cookbook* by Catherine Kitcho. It lists recipes by grouping them according to single ingredients. Stuck with some leftover tomato? You'll find multiple recipes to make with it. Stumped with what to do with that surplus of garden veggies? You'll discover dozens of dishes here. This book is worth the price simply by virtue of the money you'll cease wasting by cooking from it!

Finding Your Groove

If you are new to cooking or just haven't ever quite found your groove when it comes to organization in the kitchen, be patient. You'll eventually discover a routine that works for you and fits your lifestyle.

This is how cooking usually goes at my house. I like to make Sunday dinners from scratch, and we often have guests. Now, I don't mind admitting to you that at times we simply pick up a few $5 pizzas on the way home from church, add a salad and ice cream sandwiches, and call it good! The point, remember, is to open your home, not to impress with your fancy foodstuff fare. Simple and store-bought is just fine too.

On the days that I do cook a Sunday dinner from scratch, I usually have some leftovers. We keep Sunday evenings simple. Nacho chips and cheese or a veggie and fruit plate with assorted dips are fine for us.

On Mondays we have our biggest "stay home and crack the books" school day. We usually don't go anywhere, except that my daughter treks off to an algebra class in the afternoon. So the beginning of the week is a great day for me to make some homemade multigrain or French bread and some soup using leftovers from our Sunday supper. If after church we dined on roasted garlic chicken, potatoes, and sweet corn, we can use the leftovers to make cheesy chicken corn chowder. If I served a roast and mixed veggies, it turns into homemade vegetable beef barley soup on Monday. Turkey breast á l' orange and wild rice pilaf transforms wonderfully into wild rice and mushroom turkey soup.

On Fridays we often make homemade pizza. Saturdays often find us out and about or dining on leftovers. What about the rest of the week—Tuesdays through Thursdays? Those, dear fellow chefs, are my killer days!

During those busy three days we are running to a volley ball game in the winter or a Little League baseball matchup in the spring and summer (although we really limit our kids' activities). I know many of you have schedules that are even more hectic. But I'm going to suggest to you a method that has saved my sanity and helped me put more energy into cooking for guests because my own family's meals have gone so much smoother.

On those midweek days, I like to simply walk to the freezer and ask myself, "What will it be tonight? Mexican? Italian? Good ol' meat and potatoes?" What have I done? Spent a fortune at the local food warehouse on family-sized frozen entrees? Won a year's worth of main dishes from the local Schwan's man?

Nope. I've become a believer in freezer cooking.

Now, before you tune me out, please hear me out. I'm not talking about the "once a month" cooking concept that scares many potential would-be cooks away—the one where you spend an entire day making thirty different and complicated recipes. Nor am I speaking of bland "glop on rice" casseroles that remind you of a church potluck gone sour. I am talking about hearty and tasty main dishes that freeze well, reheat beautifully, and are family-pleasing favorites. Can't be done, you say?

While speaking at a Hearts at Home moms' conference, I became acquainted with one of the founders of the "30 Day Gourmet" freezer manual and website (www.30daygourmet.com). Although there are many great freezer cookbooks out there, this one is my favorite. The two authors have seven children combined. The meals are yummy and kid friendly. When making multiple numbers of any of the recipes, all of the math has already been done for you. This way when tripling a meal you don't need to rack your brain to figure out, "Now what is three times 2¾ cups?"

In addition to main dishes, there are sides, breads and muffins, desserts, snacks, and even breakfast sandwiches. And there are many ways to use this book. You can simply use it as a cookbook. When you are cooking a meal for your family, double it and freeze one for later. My friend and mentor Elise Arndt told me early on, "In the kitchen, be smart. Cook once; eat twice!"

You can also set aside one Saturday morning a month to make six or eight main dishes to make use of on your busiest days that month. You can start a cooking co-op, much like the familiar Christmas cookie exchanges that take place each year. Find four or five friends who will each make the same number of main dishes at home. Assign a different agreed-upon dish for each gal. Each of you simply makes and freezes your dishes, and then you all get together and swap so you each go home with the same number and type of dishes. You have a wonderful variety, but each of you only needed to make one kind. Making multiples of one entree is so much easier than switching gears (and recipes) several times to turn out an assortment. If you'd like more information on starting your own freezer swap, check out www.cookingamongfriends.com.

It is a wonderful place to start. (A side note: both the 30 Day Gourmet and Cooking Among Friends will help you with the nuts and bolts of freezer cooking such as what to freeze and not to freeze, how to use space by using one- and two-gallon bags and freezing them flat, and how to do this if you don't own an extra freezer.)

You can go another route and do as my friend Carmen and I have often done. Pick your family's four or five favorite chicken, beef, and vegetarian meals. Get together with a friend and get the children involved in something fun (or if they are really little, hire a teen to watch them for the day). Come with your meat already cooked in Crock-Pots and roasters the day before and have an assembly day. You can make the meals for your own clan or, if you are compatible cooks, combine your efforts, each taking home the same dishes in the same amount at the end of the day.

The last time Carmen and I did this, we met for coffee and planned on a Thursday afternoon. The next week we shopped separately on Wednesday, cooked our chicken and browned our beef at home on Thursday, and met and assembled our meals at Carmen's home on Friday while Mackenzie watched all six kids. At the end of our time, Carmen and I each had in our possession 90 main dish meals, 30 breakfast sandwiches, and 24 bags of bread machine dough mix for making cinnamon rolls, pizza, or focaccia bread. There were many repeats in the batch. Neither Carmen's family nor mine minds having a favorite dish a couple of times a month.

At the end of that day, we looked over our spoil like a hunter returning from the kill. Sure, we were tired. Yeah, our feet hurt. Of course we insisted that our husbands take us out for dinner that night after we'd spent all that time in the kitchen. But oh, the peace that followed!

We made those meals the third week of August, before we each launched into our homeschool year. With my normally "from scratch" Sundays, soup and bread Mondays, and easy week-ends, those meals lasted our family until March! By then, spring was coming and my busy schooling and speaking schedule was winding down. I was ready for a season of daily cooking, slow-simmering special sauces, and a lot of marinating and grilling during the warm months.

Now, please don't think you need to hog-tie a friend into agreeing to make 90 meals for each of you! Start small.

Another benefit of having meals in the freezer is that it enables you to have a "blessing meal" at your fingertips ready to take to a family that has just had a baby, has moved into your neighborhood, or perhaps is weathering a storm of life. Haven't we all heard of just such situations? They tug at our heartstrings, but when we think of running to the supermarket, cooking, and delivering a meal, it all seems so overwhelming that we simply opt out. Having a blessing meal means you simply walk to your freezer and pull out your completed menu of delicious food. (My favorite standby is a pan of Italian stuffed shells, a bag of garden sweet corn, homemade garlic breadsticks, and a strawberry cheesecake. Add a bag of salad and you have a complete and nutritious meal. If you don't use this standby after a few months, you can always feed it to your own family. Then on your next cooking day, replenish your freezer.)

Whether you commit to being a freezer cook or not, make it your aim to willingly open up your home to nourish both the bodies and the souls of those whom God will bring your way. As best you can, be ready for unexpected company, like a drop-by friend in need of a word of encouragement doled out over a favorite drink. Have cookie dough balls in the freezer ready to be baked. Slice lemons and store them in a baggie or plant a pot of mint and place it in the windowsill so you can snip off a sprig to serve with water. Peel some veggies and whip up a little dill dip. Have it ready should a neighbor stop by for a chat.

Expect God to bring others to your home. If he sees your heart is willing, he is more than able. Turn on the teakettle, start the sauce a-simmering. We've said it before, and you're almost ready: company's a-comin'!

ᔆWelcome Ideasᔆ

Turtles in My Dish Drainer

I wish I could get married all over again. Now, don't get me wrong. I'd still choose the same groom. I'd even pick out the same off-the-shoulder, ivory wedding dress. And I've never seen a ring I love more than my custom-made, heart-shaped, half-carat solitaire. No, what I'd like to do all over again is to relive the day my groom-to-be and I visited the bridal registry.

I remember it well. We met halfway between the Christian college I was still attending and the small town where he'd accepted a position as a youth pastor. Heading up the escalator at the JCPenney store in Kalamazoo, Michigan, I was filled with excitement. How fun it would be to choose linens, dishes, and décor for the little one-bedroom apartment we'd soon call home.

We pored over the various patterns and styles in the housewares department. I was elated when he agreed to the dishes I'd had my heart set on and the colors I wanted for the bathroom, kitchen, and living room. We discussed comforters and candlesticks, shower curtains and sheets. But as the minutes turned to hours, my once-cheerful fiancé sat slumped on the floor with his back up against the side of a toaster display, mumbling, "I don't care anymore . . . just pick something!" As a male, he didn't find the same exhilaration in this activity as I did. I had dreamed of this day for months! We'd select exactly what items we wanted in our humble home. Then well-wishing friends and family members would happily pay for them. What a setup! What I didn't realize, however, was that these items wouldn't be for my husband and I alone to use and enjoy. As they say, first comes love, then comes marriage . . . well, you know the rest.

Now three children and twenty years later, I wish I could choose my items all over again. Who would've ever imagined where some of those possessions would one day end up? If I'd known then what I know now . . . well, here are some of the choices I would have made differently:

Our state-of-the-art, stainless steel pasta colander. Instead of asking myself, "Is this big enough to hold spaghetti noodles for a party of twelve?" I should have pondered the question, "Will this, when turned upside down and placed in our garden, be able to accommodate our son Spencer's pet toad Hoppy and six of his closest kin, providing shelter while still allowing them to breathe?"

Our 200-thread-count, full-size floral cotton sheet set. Instead of making sure it matched our comforter and complemented our bedroom colors, I should have given it this test: "Will it still be in good enough shape ten years from now to be made into a tablecloth and napkin set for our five-year-old Mackenzie's Victorian tea table?"

Our Revere cookware set with the copper-clad bottoms. How foolish of me to diligently research and then choose based on its ability to conduct heat on both gas and electric burners. Why was I ever swayed by their warranty plan and top-notch *Consumer Reports* rating? Rather, I should have asked myself these questions: "Are there enough different-sized pans in this ensemble to make a full drum set for eighteen-month-old Mitchell armed with two large wooden soup spoons? And will it stand the test of time as the instrument of choice for three different drum-crazed children?" Thank goodness for their lifetime warranty!

Our beautiful silver cake server with the real ivory handle. This one hurts! Here I envisioned cutting our beautiful wedding cake. Then we'd bring this fine piece of cutlery out of storage year after year only for special anniversaries and important milestones. I never dreamed where it would one day end up. Here's what I should have contemplated instead: "Will this be the perfect fit for a four-year-old's makeshift belt, instantly turning him into Peter Pan, ready to take on Captain Hook with his (as he puts it) 'trusty sword' by his side?"

Our dish drainer. Not much thought went into that decision. I just chose one based on our colors. I should have, however, given thought to this: "Will this be large enough to properly drain fourteen small rubber snakes, six plastic frogs, and four snapping turtles from the dollar store after my five-year-old is finished playing with them in the bathtub?"

Well, there you have it. Thankfully our crystal goblets and cut glass bowls are safely locked up in the china hutch. Otherwise, who knows what disaster might have befallen them? Just the other day my boys wondered how many shots from a Red Ryder BB gun it might take to shatter real glass instead of the simple cardboard targets they now use. I should have gone for the Tupperware!

Cooking for a Crowd

Let's face it, if you want to be well practiced in the area of offering hospitality to larger groups of people, you are just going to have to learn to cook for a crowd. Here's how:

First, make friends with your Crock-Pot or slow cooker. Go buy one if you don't have one. This is the single most important tool for making large and easy meals. I actually own three. I can make our main dish in one, peeled cooked potatoes in the second, and a dessert in the third.

Invest in some quality cookware: large roasters, cookie sheets and jelly roll pans, a few good 9-by-13 pans, a couple large stock pots and soup kettles, etc. I prefer stainless steel or enamelware. Nonstick ones don't last very long. And as with most things, you get what you pay for.

Forget the fine china. Invest in a nice set of Corelle dishes instead. They are inexpensive and lightweight, take up much less space than traditional stoneware, and come in many pretty patterns. Or try plain white so you can decorate your table around them no matter the season. My friend Carmen actually bought some clear dinner plates from the local dollar store to use for company. For added fun, she can place fall leaves, photographs, and other items underneath them to show through, adding to the décor.

Learn to make simple food, but plenty of it. Many gals in my survey stressed that fancy food was not important. But having delicious, simple food and enough of it to go around was.

Get kid-friendly. Find some recipes that will be hits with kids. Or if you insist on some fun, fancy fare for the adults, make sure you supplement it with something children will enjoy.

Think in themes. Theme dinners are usually a hit. Hold a Mexican night or serve Chinese. Cook several shapes of pasta and serve them with an assortment of sauces, a tossed salad, and bread hot from the oven. Give guests small plates to pour on olive oil, fresh grated garlic, and a little basil or oregano for dipping. Or have a 1950s night with burgers, fries, and malts or soda pop. Get creative!

The Nuts and Bolts

Here are some well-tested sample menus that are sure to please your guests. Remember to try them on your family first!

Teena Sand contributed these first two recipe ideas:

Cranberry and Feta Cheese Salad

8 cups mixed greens (iceberg, romaine, garden,
    bib, whatever you have on hand)
8 ounces feta cheese crumbles
1 cup chopped walnuts

1 cup dried cranberries (can substitute
mandarin oranges, sliced canned pears, or
fresh strawberries)

Mix dressing at least one hour before serving. Dressing:

¼ cup white vinegar
½ cup olive oil
⅓ cup sugar
¼ cup finely minced sweet onion
½ teaspoon salt
½ teaspoon dried mustard
dash pepper

Toss salad with dressing just before serving. The sweet flavor of the dressing combined with the feta makes for an interesting combination. People who ordinarily don't like feta usually do like this salad.

Cheese and Herb Stuffed Chicken

6 boneless, skinless chicken breasts
1 small tub flavored cream cheese (garlic and
herb, chive and onion, or garden vegetable)
1 cup dried bread crumbs
2 tablespoons parmesan cheese
4 tablespoons melted butter or margarine

Flatten chicken breasts inside a gallon Ziploc bag using a meat mallet or a soup can. Place 1 tablespoon cream cheese in center of each breast, roll up, and secure with toothpicks. Dip breasts first in butter and then in a mixture of bread crumbs and parmesan. Place in a greased 9-by-13 pan and bake at 350 for approximately 35 minutes or until done. Serves 6.

Julie Gill shares these awesome homemade crescent rolls. They are so easy and delicious!

Never-Fail Rolls

1 package yeast
1½ cups warm water
3¼ cups flour
½ teaspoon salt
1 9-ounce (Jiffy) cake mix, either yellow or white
melted butter

Dissolve yeast in warm water. Mix in all ingredients except butter. Do NOT knead. Put in greased large bowl and let it rise until doubled or about 1 hour. Punch down, divide into two, and roll out into two 12-inch circles. Divide into 12 triangles each and roll into crescent rolls. Put each dozen on greased cookie sheets and let rise about 25 minutes. Bake at 350 degrees for 12–15 minutes or until browned. Remove from oven and brush with melted butter. These also freeze and reheat well so that you can make them ahead. Makes 24 rolls.

Here's another one of Julie's recipes for a great side dish. When she takes this to family or church gatherings, she always runs out, and many people ask for the recipe.

Corn Casserole

1 can creamed corn
1 can whole corn (drained)
8 ounces sour cream
⅓ cup sugar
½ cup vegetable oil
2 eggs, lightly beaten
8½ ounce box Jiffy corn muffin mix

Mix all together and pour into a 2½ quart baking dish. Bake at 350 for 45 minutes to 1 hour. Serves 4–6. (Julie usually doubles the recipe to fill a 9-by-13-inch pan and extends the baking time.)

This next one is a delightful warm-up on a crisp fall or snowy winter day.

Hot Fruit Compote

20-ounce can pineapple chunks
2 15-ounce cans peach slices
15-ounce can pear slices
2 10-ounce jars maraschino cherries
2 15-ounce cans mandarin oranges
⅓ cup sugar
4 tablespoons cornstarch
½ cup corn syrup
1 cup orange juice
1 teaspoon vanilla

Drain fruit, reserving pineapple and peach juice. Arrange fruit in 9-by-13 pan. Mix remainder of ingredients except vanilla with 1 cup reserved juices. Heat to a boil, stirring constantly. Remove from heat and add vanilla. Pour over fruit. Bake uncovered at 350 degrees for 30 minutes. Serve warm. For the deluxe version, serve over a slice of pound cake topped with a scoop of vanilla ice cream. Serves 8.

This refreshing and easy meal starter was contributed by Elizabeth Bruick.

Cool Spring Salad

4 cups torn iceberg lettuce
4 cups torn leaf lettuce
1 cup strawberries, cut into very small bites
½ cup pecans
½ cup crumbled blue cheese
¾ cup sweet poppy seed dressing

Spread pecans on cookie sheet, bake in 300 degree oven for 10 minutes, turn and bake 10 minutes more. Cool. Tear enough lettuce to fill a medium-sized bowl, top with strawberries, pecans, and blue cheese. Can refrigerate at this point till later. When ready to eat, pour dressing on top and toss all together. Refreshing!

A clever new twist on an old favorite. A crowd pleaser!

Mexican Chicken Lasagna

½ cup finely chopped onion
2 14.5-ounce cans petite diced tomatoes, drained
1¼ cup mild picante sauce
1 package taco seasoning mix
16-ounce can black beans, drained and rinsed
2 large egg whites
1 cup ricotta cheese
10 lasagna noodles, uncooked
2 cups chopped, cooked chicken
4-ounce can diced mild green chile peppers
8-ounce package shredded sharp cheddar
    cheese

Mix first four ingredients in a large bowl. Add beans, stirring lightly. In a separate bowl, mix egg whites and ricotta cheese. Spread 1½ cups of the bean sauce over the bottom of a greased 9-by-13 pan. Top with five uncooked noodles, overlapping slightly. Spread with half of the remaining sauce mixture. Sprinkle with half the chiles followed by half of the chopped chicken. Spread ricotta mixture over chicken. Sprinkle on half the cheese. Add five more noodles, the rest of the sauce, chiles, chicken, and cheese, making sure noodles are well covered. Bake uncovered at 350 degrees for 45–55 minutes until noodles are fully cooked. Cool slightly before serving. Top with sour cream, extra salsa, and chopped lettuce. Serves 8–10.

A Life That Says Welcome

Here's a sweet and easy ending to any meal. I make this seemingly fancy but actually easy cake for my friend Michelle on her birthday each August. Delicious!

Lemon Poppy Seed Bundt Cake

1 yellow cake mix
¼ cup oil
¼ cup water
⅓ cup sour cream
2 eggs
1 teaspoon almond extract
⅓ cup lemon juice
2 tablespoons poppy seeds

Glaze:
1 cup powdered sugar
3 tablespoons lemon juice

Mix all but glaze ingredients on low speed until well blended. Pour into greased and floured bundt cake pan. Bake 40 minutes at 350 degrees. Cool 10 minutes. Invert onto cake plate. Cool slightly. Combine glaze ingredients and drizzle over cake. Store covered. This is best made the day before. Delightful with a warm mug of tea!

This casserole was contributed by Marcia Stump. Children love it!

Corndog Casserole

2 tablespoons butter
1 cup green onions, chopped fine (optional)
2 pounds hot dogs, sliced into rounds
2 eggs
1½ cups milk
2 teaspoons ground sage
1 teaspoon salt
¼ teaspoon pepper
3 cups shredded cheddar cheese
2 (8½ -ounce) packages cornbread muffin mix

Sauté onions with hot dogs in butter. Set aside. Mix cornbread muffin mixes with eggs, milk, spices, and 1 ½ cups cheese. Add hot dog mixture. Spread in 3-quart casserole dish or 9-by-13 greased pan. Top with remaining cheese. Bake at 400 degrees for 30 minutes or until golden brown. Serves 6.

Tricia Brown offers this kid-friendly favorite idea.

Frito Pie—A Southern Classic

Make one recipe of your family's favorite chili. Serve over small Fritos corn chips. Top with chopped onions and shredded cheddar cheese. In the South lots of functions will actually just place a slit in the Frito bag and put the chili in—then you eat it out of the bag. This is great for company because the chili can be done in the Crock-Pot, the Fritos

A Life That Says Welcome

require no preparation, and the cheese and onions can be done the day before. Everyone always loves this, and it will feed quite a crowd on a modest budget. Kids especially love it!

Peanut Butter Pie—Another Kid-Pleasing Favorite!

> 1 9-ounce ready-made graham cracker crust, 2
>   extra serving size
> 8 ounces cream cheese
> 1½ cups powdered sugar
> ½ cup milk
> ¾ cup smooth peanut butter
> 8 ounces frozen nondairy whipped topping

Mix all but whipped topping on medium speed until smooth. Gently fold in whipped topping and spread into pie crust. Wrap in foil or plastic wrap. Freeze until solid. To serve, thaw slightly and serve with additional whipped topping (or for the deluxe version add hot fudge too!).

The Cookbook Corner

Invest in a few good resources that will give you appetizing ideas for all aspects of your meal. Here are a few of my favorites:

- Any of the Gooseberry Patch cookbooks. These offer recipes from home chefs across the country—ones that are simple and tasty too!

- *Taste of Home* magazine. Again, recipes are from women all over the country, regular cooks just like you. I have yet to try a recipe from *Taste of Home* that hasn't been a hit!

- *The Silver Palate Cookbook.* My mother-in-law gave me this book years ago. If you do want to go somewhat gourmet, this is the book for you. Wonderful recipes and clear instructions will transform almost any home chef into a culinary genius!

- *The Freezer Manual from 30 Day Gourmet.* The best resource for cooking meals ahead and freezing them for later use. Saves you time and money and helps you to concentrate your efforts on having your heart and home ready. Don't worry about the meal. It's in the freezer! Available at www.30daygourmet .com.

- *Cooking Among Friends* by Mary Tennant and Becki Visser, available from www.cookingamongfriends.com. Another great freezer cooking resource. This book also walks you through setting up a freezer swap cooking group.

- *Miserly Meals* by Jonni McCoy. A budget-conscious volume full of great main and side dish ideas, make-ahead mixes, and wonderful desserts. You'll save the price of the book in no time flat!

8

Here Is the Church, Here Is the Steeple, Open Your Hearts and Bless All the People

A while back while teaching a workshop on de-stressing your Sundays, I wrote this poem comparing two families. Read it and see if you can relate:

> "I can't find my socks!" the young boy cried, his voice
> filled with despair.
> "And I've lost my Bible," his sister chimed. "Can't find it
> anywhere!"
>
> "Mom, what's to eat?" the toddler cried, still in his little
> p.j.'s.
> "I don't know," his mom replied. "I haven't bought gro-
> ceries for days!"

Dad soon got up, wandered down the hall, "Hey honey
    . . . where's my tie?"
"Don't ask me now, I'm ironing," came mother's sharp
    reply.

The baby then woke, some milk got spilled, a fight broke
    out between two.
Dad burnt the toast, brother flipped on the TV—oh,
    what's a mom to do?

Arising late this family found chaos at every turn,
Each Sunday morning this same scene played—you'd
    think they would have learned!

Finally at the church safe and sound but stressed out to
    the max—
Wishing the service would soon be done so they could go
    home and relax.

But returning home they found a mess, the house now
    out of order,
And with no food Dad soon had to make a quick "run for
    the border"!

The rest of the day was catch-up time—where was the
    Lord in this?
On this, his day, did he have a plan this family com-
    pletely missed?

Across the street that very same day, another family
    arose,
But something was different, for at this house here's how
    their Sunday goes:

"I've got my Bible," the young boy cried; his voice was
    filled with glee.
"And I've packed the diaper bag," his sister chimed.
    "Does anyone else need me?"

"Yeah—cinnamon rolls!" the toddler cried, dressed in his
   Sunday best.
The family joined hands and blessed the food, inviting
   Christ to be their guest.

Each put on their clothes and gathered their things while
   from the CD player
Arose songs of praise and thanksgiving and choruses
   filled with prayer.

Soon out the door and on their way, they talked of the
   service to come—
The fellowship, the new truths of God—oh, how they
   longed for some!

When church was done, a new family they met and invited them home to eat,
No fear of returning to a messy house did they have
   when approaching their street.

They opened the door and from the kitchen came a most
   glorious smell.
The table was set, and dessert had been made—no need
   here for Taco Bell!

After a lovely meal with their newfound friends, the kids
   gladly napped for they knew
That the rest of the day would be focused on God, with
   so many fun things to do!

At the close of the day, when tucking all in, these parents
   were thrilled to see
Once again Sunday brought them closer to God—the way
   it's supposed to be.

Now, let me ask you, ladies so dear—yes, a quick quiz
   now I'll give—
When it comes to your Sundays, God's most special day,
In which house do you live?

Well, ladies . . . I am here to tell you that I have lived in both!

When we were first parents, Sundays at our house were a blur. Getting up late, dragging ourselves to church, and then spending the rest of the day tackling piles of laundry, bill paying, housework, and any other task we'd not gotten done during the week. To us, Sundays were "catch-up day," for two reasons, really: not only did we catch up on work not done during the week, but "ketchup" was the only food I served to go along with the hamburgers and French fries we got at the fast-food drive-through!

The scene at your house may be different. Perhaps you don't have young children underfoot or any children in the house at all, but my experience has been that most women have pretty harried Sundays. As a result, we often miss out on a prime opportunity to offer hospitality to others and to the Lord each Sunday.

Yeah, you heard me right. I said, "to the Lord."

Here we can take a cue from the way our Jewish brothers and sisters treat the Sabbath in their families. My first exposure to this was when in college I saw a magnificent production of the musical *Fiddler on the Roof*. There I peered into the home of a Jewish family for the first time. Let me tell you about the Sabbath depicted there for a moment.

Just before sundown, a hustle and bustle of activity and expectation hung thick in the air as the family rushed around, readying themselves for the holy day to come. The chores were done; the food was prepared; special dishes to be used only on the Sabbath were carefully placed on the table. The children dropped coins in a box to be given later to the poor. One of the daughters ran to the window to check the position of the setting sun. Then just as the sun finished its final descent, the family members took their places at the table. The mother of the house then lit two candles: one to remember the Sabbath, one to keep it holy. At that point a little bell rang as the announcement was made that "Queen

Sabbath" had arrived—the special guest they have been getting ready for all week.

I've since turned to research and resources that highlight the Old Testament observation of the Sabbath to learn more. I found that at this stage in their celebration, Jewish families then greet each other by saying "Shabbat Shalom." They are wishing each other "Sabbath peace." Then they are off to attend a Friday evening service at the synagogue. Returning home, the father blesses each of his children by laying his hands on their head. We find this practice described in Numbers 6:24–27. He also blesses his wife by quoting verses from Proverbs 31 about the wife of noble character. (Oh, wouldn't that be wonderful! Most of us would do well to begin to speak to our family members about their admirable traits and stop reminding them of their flaws!)

Then the family pronounces the kiddush, which is a prayer recited over wine and two loaves of challah bread, a sweet, braided loaf. Time to eat the Sabbath meal! This consists of chicken soup, fish, beef, and beautiful pastries that are kept under a special cloth until ready to be revealed. Then the family is off to bed.

The following morning finds them up early attending a morning service followed by a time of "noshing" where they snack and enjoy fellowship with each other. (Hmm, where we get our Sunday coffee and cookie hour, perhaps?)

Returning home, they are allowed to nap, read, and eat, but not to perform any work. Finally the family attends a late afternoon service where the rabbi pronounces the havdalah prayer over wine and spices and a braided havdalah candle. *Havdalah* means division. The idea here is that they as a congregation are now dividing up and returning back to their weekly lives once again. The service is short and sweet, and there is actually sadness that the day is over and that Queen Sabbath is leaving until the next Sabbath. Forty minutes after sundown, it is all over.

Now, this was serious business. If you as a Jew were to violate the most holy day of the year, Yom Kippur, the Day of Atonement, you were faced with excommunication from the congregation. But do you know what happened to you if you failed to properly observe the Sabbath? You were put to death! The first time you were warned. The next time you faced fistfuls of rocks flying at you as you were stoned to death.

Of course, as Christians we no longer observe the Sabbath in the way laid out for us in the Old Testament. Most Christians worship corporately on what is called the Lord's Day, which is held on Sunday, the first day of the week, not on the traditional seventh day, Saturday. Why the switch?

Biblical scholars trace this back to the fact that Jesus rose from the dead on the first day of the week, which was Sunday. The change for early Christians presumably took place during the forty days before the ascension. Acts 20:7 says that the early church came together on the first day of the week to share fellowship and break bread.

Even though we are no longer bound to observe the Sabbath in an Old Testament manner, are there lessons we can learn and concepts we can glean from our Jewish brothers and sisters? You betcha!

First of all, let me say that when my husband and I were first parents, our Sundays were a mess. They were not a day of delight as Isaiah 58:13 says the Sabbath is to be. They were a day of dread and disaster! But slowly God began to teach us that the tide could be turned if we were willing to listen and make some changes by taking our cues from the Jews.

Take the way they plan for the Sabbath. It doesn't just sneak up on them unnoticed as Sunday does on many Christian families: "Oh my! Is it time to go to church already? The laundry isn't done, this house is a mess, and I have nothing at all planned for our noon meal!" If the Jewish people delight in welcoming

Queen Sabbath each week, how much more should we anticipate the arrival of King Jesus! If he were coming in the flesh to your house next Sunday, why, you'd be ready, wouldn't you? You'd never dream of folding laundry, cleaning your bathroom, or sorting through your junk mail instead of visiting with him, would you? You'd never park him on the couch and dash off to tackle some trivial pursuit, all the while ignoring the Master sitting in your midst. Sadly, that is what a lot of us do each week.

But take heart! We can learn to reorder our weeks, making Sunday a day to worship and welcome the Lord and others into our home and the rest of the week a time to tackle our household tasks, yard work, and other responsibilities of life.

But where to start? Well, work backwards. If you want your Sunday schedule cleared, begin by using the days leading up to it to finish your work. Say on Thursday you are going to deal with your piles. Come on, I know you have them. We all do. Put those papers away and pitch the ones you do not need. No, you do not need another credit card. Don't even open the application.

Let's move on. Perhaps Friday can serve as a laundry and de-cluttering day. Get that place picked up before you hit the sack. Then you can wake up to a house that is ready to be rid of dirt and grime. The whole family can pitch in and do some speed cleaning. Prepare for your Sunday meal as much as you can on Saturday. Ready yourself and your family for the following day. Lay out clothes, pack the diaper bag, even set the table for your noon meal before retiring on Saturday. (For Sunday breakfast, you can eat on paper plates.)

Are you getting the picture? I don't want to be a legalist in any way. I am not suggesting that it is a sin to do any work on Sunday. I am not saying you absolutely can't fold that laundry, or take a shopping trip, or do anything else you may choose to do on the Lord's Day.

I have had to chuckle over the years as I have seen the various ways different families treat the Sabbath. One day I was sitting in our church's nursery rocking a baby during a service. At the time I was developing a workshop on making Sundays a family day of delight. I decided to poll the moms present to see what they thought about various aspects of my talk. When I came to the issue of whether or not to perform any work on Sunday, opinions began to fly.

One woman piped up, "Oh, we have very strong guidelines when it comes to working on Sundays. We simply believe it is wrong. In fact, we never even go out to eat on Sundays because that would mean that the chef and the waitress would have to work in order to serve us our meal."

No sooner had she taken her infant and exited the nursery than my friend Trisha began to snicker. "What is so funny?" I asked.

She regained her composure and then announced, "Oh, David and I are very strict about not working on Sundays. In fact, he never lets me cook or wash dishes. We always go out to eat!"

Again, I am not attempting to tell you just what your family can and cannot do on Sundays. That is strictly between you and God. I am merely saying that with a little planning and perseverance, if you desire Sundays to be a day of rest, worship, and welcome, it is totally doable! Again, if we can do it, then you most certainly can!

Setting Apart Sundays

The Jews were told to remember the Sabbath and to keep it holy. The Hebrew word for holy means set apart or different. How can Sundays at your house be different from the rest of the week? For us it meant that Sundays were the day we would invite others over for a meal and an afternoon visit.

Oh, let me tell you, when we first started doing this on a regular basis, I was shaking in my boots. Sure, we had entertained others for a meal here and there. I was getting good at blessing others "on the road" with little heartfelt gifts or lovingly baked treats. I could even have my in-laws over for a night's stay and not freak out (well, not *totally* freak out!). But to have other families over from the new church we had just started attending? That seemed a bit daunting to me.

Well, thankfully, God gave me enough courage to start with just one family. I didn't know at the time why he chose this particular family and placed the desire to have them over on my heart, but I do now. They are about the most real and transparent couple you ever could meet, and anything I cooked or served seemed to delight them to no end.

Yep, our new friends Duane and Renee were our first hospitality guinea pigs. We would invite them along with their then three (and now five) children over for Sunday supper when we were new at our church. I'd try my best to make a decent and delicious meal. I'd let Renee bring along something if she liked. Before I had insisted that every single item on the table be made by my compliment-hungry little hands. I have since learned that it is a huge blessing to the hostess and a pleasure to the guest if they bring along part of the meal. Of course I don't ask them to, but if they offer, I certainly take them up on it.

After church we'd let the dads discuss in the living room and the kids play in the backyard or bedroom while Renee and I put the finishing touches on the meal. Then we'd call them all to the table.

Uh, oops . . . not enough room at the table.

Remember, this was the kitchen where even at full capacity, we only had room for four. So we improvised. The four adults ate in the kitchen, and the kids ate in the living room on a plastic children's picnic table that had been placed on top of a blanket in order to catch the crumbs. If one of us had a baby at the time, he or she was placed in the high chair in the tiny mudroom entryway that was immediately adjacent to our little kitchen.

Reflecting back on that time in our family's life, I can't tell you how afraid and embarrassed I was to have to cram company in like that. But in retrospect I can honestly tell you that these memories are among my most treasured, for it was then that we learned some important truths about true Christian hospitality.

You see, people don't care if they are a bit crowded if they can sense the love of Christ. They can still feel warm and welcomed in a small home as long as the hosts have big hearts. Remember, "Ven there is vroom in your heart. . . ." If anything, they will applaud you for your courage and ingenuity as you turn your petite place into a center of nourishment and refreshment.

Yes, Sundays for us became a treasured time of hospitality. For months we practiced on Duane and Renee. It became almost a tradition, and as I said, they were always so encouraging about the food I provided. Now, over a decade later, on his birthday each spring I still make Duane a pan of Boston Grahams, his favorite dessert (recipe later in this chapter).

After practicing on the Schafers, we began to branch out. On many Sundays during the year you would find a different family, couple, or single seated around that small antique kitchen table (or if it was a family with many kids, out in our backyard in the summer eating picnic style, our solution to our somewhat limited space).

Yes, God used our willingness to cease from our work and make our Sundays set apart to provide us with the perfect time to offer hospitality to other Christians or visitors to our church. So many of the dear folks we consider lifelong friends now were merely strangers to us before that first invitation to supper. Whom is God calling you to reach out to with an invite for Sunday dinner? Don't list the excuses why it won't work. Get ready. Anticipate. Prepare and provide. God will bring along someone that he knows needs the refreshment and fun only your family can offer that day.

Your job? Be on the lookout for just such a soul. Get your kids in on the act. Let them occasionally make suggestions about who at church might enjoy a home-cooked meal, a pizza from the parlor, or even a bucket of chicken from the Colonel if you so desire.

I was hesitant to ask others to join us for dinner when our kids were younger for fear that they might not behave as little angels. What joy we nearly missed! We have delighted to see our kids develop love for widows, shut-ins, and others who are in desperate need of some human contact—even the rowdy, rambunctious, kid kind. Often when we had an elderly person over when our children were small, I fretted over the activity level of my offspring during the visit. God in his gracious way often saw fit for me to receive a glowing report back about the visit. Once a friend at church told me what a delightful time a widow had during a recent Sunday visit. "Really?" I responded, assuming she was only attempting to appear polite.

"Oh yes," my friend replied. "She said she simply loved watching your boys playing heartily at her feet and enjoyed your daughter climbing up into her lap to have a story read. She can't remember when she felt such a part of a young, vibrant family! I sure hope you have her over again real soon!"

Shame on me. The very behaviors I thought would be annoying to these dear saints were in reality a delight instead. Trust me. Many who live alone are absolutely thrilled when they can be a part of a family for a day, even if your day is a rather ordinary one.

Making the Switch

Now, I would never want to give you the impression that our weeks always operate flawlessly and smoothly. Sundays are still sometimes stressful. We still have loose ends, lost shoes, misplaced Bibles, and an occasional burnt roast (the preacher's fault, not mine—just kidding!).

What has changed for us is the percentage of time we reside in each of the houses described in my poem at the top of this chapter. When we began our quest, we were family number one 99 percent of the time. Every once in a while, with great late-night effort on my part, we could pull off a decent meal or have someone over for an evening dessert without the house looking too shabby.

Now, after much practice at reordering our week, we have taken up residence in the second house. No, not 100 percent of the time, but a majority of the time. And it has been well worth the effort. Do you realize that if you truly set out to make Sundays a day of rest and worship at your house, it is like taking fifty-two mini-vacations a year with time off from your usual workweek? Of course, you don't need to have company all fifty-two times, but certainly you could manage say, once a month. At the end of a year, you would have blessed twelve individuals or families by opening your home.

The rest of the time, focus on offering welcome to your own family. Relax. Converse. Play a board game. Take a walk. Read a book aloud. Celebrate the blessed ordinary.

And don't forget to offer welcome to the Lord. He isn't just that unseen guest at your Sunday supper table. He is present throughout the entire day. Determine not to let him go ignored any longer.

❧Welcome Ideas☙

Offering Welcome to the Lord:
Your Special Spot

We can have a special spot set aside in our home where we can meet with the Lord not only on Sundays but throughout the week. Some have a favorite chair, a cozy spot in front of the fireplace, or a sunny location out on the back porch where they can read the Bible, ponder, and pray. When choosing such a spot, consider these points.

❧ Pick a place where it will be quiet when you want to have your quiet time—imagine that! A place out in the flow of traffic doesn't work well during midday.

❧ If you are using a little corner of a family or living room, choose a comfortable chair or love seat. Make sure the lighting is adequate. Have needed items nearby and ready to go—Bible, pen, journal, and so on. If the Lord calls you any time of the day or night, you can simply go to your spot and meet with him.

❧ Consider having a CD player with worshipful CDs so you can play them to get yourself in the right frame of mind.

❧ Have a pad of paper or "to do" list nearby. This doesn't sound very spiritual. However, if you are like me and your mind can wander easily, having a paper where you can jot down the things that pop into your mind that may distract you can be helpful. If you remember you need to cancel an appointment or pick something up at the store, somehow just getting it off of your mind and onto paper can help you refocus.

❧ If you'd like to rotate where you'll spend your quiet time, consider making a portable quiet time basket or tote bag. I can grab my quiet time bag when I want to steal away for a few minutes and go to the family room or out on the back deck. In it I keep my Bible, a journal and pen, and any Bible study book I am currently working on. I also keep some stationery, stamps, and my address book in case God prompts me to pray for a friend and then drop her an uplifting note.

Special Sunday Ideas

Develop your own unique family traditions. *Holy* means set apart, so we want our Sundays to be different from the rest of the week. Plan some activities, however simple, that will take place only on Sundays. With small children, obtain some games and toys that have a spiritual connection and are only to be played with on Sundays. Our kids enjoyed a Noah's ark set; an armor of God shield, helmet, and sword; and a children's Bible trivia game from a yard sale. Families of all ages and stages can make a tradition of taking an afternoon drive in the countryside or an evening stroll through town. Drive to a lake or park for a picnic lunch. Take another family or single person along.

Catch a quick movie. No, not at your local theater, in your home. Purchase some DVDs that will serve as your own Sunday cinema selection. Choose storylines that point to God. Perhaps a biblical epic, a portrayal of the life of a person in Scripture, a Veggie Tales DVD, or the story of a great Christian of the past such as *Chariots of Fire*, the story of Christian runner Eric Liddell and the 1924 Olympics, or *The Hiding Place*, the tale of brave Corrie ten Boom, who helped to hide Jews from the Nazis. Pop the popcorn, turn out the lights, and make a movie memory.

Spin a tale. Set aside a few minutes on Sunday afternoon for a good old-fashioned family read-aloud. Choose a biography of a missionary or great preacher from the past. Read about modern-day missionaries and the work they are doing. Pick up a work of children's Christian fiction such as one of the volumes in the Frank Peretti mystery series for kids.

Fun family do-votions. Oh, has this been fun for our family for over a decade! Utilize the wonderful resources available today that teach biblical truths by way of an object lesson or Bible science experiment. My husband and I are firm believers in the phrase, "What I hear, I forget. What I see, I remember. But what I do, I learn." Check your local Christian bookstore for these types of books.

Serve sacred food. Okay, maybe it isn't sacred, but it can be special. To further set apart Sundays as different, choose foods that are dear to your family and serve them only on Sundays. Maybe it's chocolate. Develop a repertoire of several decadent chocolate desserts and save them for Sundays. Maybe it's steak or salmon or raspberries—whatever your brood has a hankering for.

Take the Crock-Pot challenge. Years ago we implemented this simple idea. Fill a slow cooker with a yummy hot meal. Add some simple sides—a salad, a veggie, or simple baked potatoes and dessert. Go to church on the lookout for a family or individual that could use a home-cooked meal and some pleasant company. You can implement the same idea without a slow cooker if you have a timed bake oven where you can set it to click on while you are at church so you return home to a delicious and not overdone meal.

Connect with other Christians worldwide. We have made it a point ever since our first child was a tot to expose our children to the church in all cultures. It isn't enough to just attend a missions-minded church. We need to personally model love for all of God's people—those from every nation, tribe, and tongue. Here are a couple of our favorite resources.

Voice of the Martyrs magazine and website (www.persecution .com) has resources for teaching your children about the persecuted church. No, it's not pretty, but we feel it is important for our children to know just what other Christians around the world have to endure while we in America can worship so freely. Their resource Kids of Courage cites stories of courageous children from foreign countries. They also have many hands-on projects your family can participate in, such as Blankets of Love, collecting new or gently used blankets to send to persecuted Christians in foreign lands.

Window on the World by Daphne Spraggett with Jill Johnstone is a wonderful hardcover reference volume that is loaded with full-color pictures and interesting facts about nations and people groups around the world. Each section contains ideas for how to pray for people of that particular culture.

Bring the church into your home. Use your home to further the gospel. Offer it for a youth event for the young folks at your church. Let the couples' Bible study meet in your living room. Host your own Bible study for neighbors who may not yet know Christ. When our family has done this, we have seen dear neighbors come to Christ and then become strong, active members of a local church. A wonderful resource to check out is Neighborhood Bible Studies (www.neighborhoodbiblestudy.org). They have great studies written for those not yet familiar with Scripture. We have used these in our neighborhood as well as several times in my husband's workplace at a factory with great success.

Host fellow believers. Make your home available for missionaries, speakers, singers, and actors visiting to take part in your church's worship service. We have been blessed to house such servants over the years. The stories of faith that our children get to hear are better than anything Hollywood can dream up. The first time we did this, our three-year-old daughter delighted in the antics of the "Balloon Man," a visiting Christian magician who illustrated the story of Jonah and the whale with colorful twisted balloons.

Adopt a single. Scripture says that "God sets the lonely in families" (Ps. 68:6). Perhaps your family can take on this important ministry. Many singles feel left out at church. Sunday can be a long and lonely day for them. Invite them to supper. Take them to a park to watch your kids play while you visit. Let them use your washer and dryer (laundromats are lonely places). Blend them into your family. We have been blessed to have many college students over and to permanently "adopt" a dear saint in our church named Dona Beth, a single gal living alone in our small town. We are fortunate enough to be one of four families with the privilege of "running Dona Beth," as we call it. Unable to drive, she often needs us to take her to the store or a doctor's appointment. My husband serves as handyman or painter for her home. We'll take her with us to a child's event. Or sometimes we simply stop by for a visit. Mackenzie likes to see what needlework project she is working on. The boys like to pester her cat. Dona Beth loves every minute of it, and our family is blessed to know this saint with an unwavering faith in God and love for his people.

Rejoice and weep. Take to heart the Bible's admonition to rejoice with those who rejoice and weep with those who weep. Be there with food in hand during periods of both happiness and crisis in the lives of your fellow Christians. These times are opportunities to serve as Christ's hands and feet to those believers in your corner of the world. On a larger scale, use your home as a center of blessing during such times. When a woman in our small group was facing an unwanted divorce, we invited nearly twenty women to our home for a special prayer meeting on her behalf. Later, when enduring the fallout from this sad time in her life, we held a big surprise birthday party for her. During all of this time, our basement family room and nearby guest bathroom served as a home away from home for her as she traveled to our town to transport her kids to their father's house.

Support the secretaries. On Secretary's Day, don't forget your church's secretaries. They help keep things operating smoothly all year. Take them a bouquet of flowers or a light snack and perhaps a hand-painted picture from one of your children.

Crash your deacons' meeting. Wouldn't they just flip if you showed up with a plate of goodies and a heartfelt thank-you? No list of complaints. No grumbling. Just a simple gesture to show your appreciation for the work they do on behalf of the Lord.

Drop a line. Make a habit of writing a simple note each week to someone you encountered at church. Did you sit in front of someone who sang beautiful harmony on the hymns? Did a timid teen play piano for the offering? Send them a note of encouragement.

Enlarge your borders. Consider offering hospitality to an often forgotten segment of our society—foreign exchange students. Approximately 600,000 students are presently studying in our country. Over 80 percent of these will return to their homeland to take up positions of leadership in government, education, and business. Most of them are here for four or more years, yet 70 percent of them never see the inside of an American's home. Shame on us! Many of them would love to be invited over for a home-cooked meal and to have a chance to practice their English on a real American family. A great majority of these scholars are from countries within the "10/40 Window" such as India, Cambodia, Saudi Arabia, and Japan. Modern missions has focused its efforts on these countries. We have them in our own backyards! Contact your local university or a church in a university town with a ministry to these students. See how you can link up with these folks. Offer to take them to a ball game or have them over for a meal or an evening. Expose your children to someone from another culture in the comfort of your own home. Our friends the Leifs have done this over the years. Their children have enjoyed getting to know firsthand the customs and practices that up until then they knew only from the pages of a textbook. They encourage us to start out small—perhaps a one-time invite for a church service and Sunday supper, then branch out from there. (Note: These statistics are from International Student Ministries, Inc., 2005, www.intervarsity.org/ism.)

Pamper the Pastor

Often we'd like to show love and respect to those who serve the Lord as clergy, but we just don't know where to start. My friend and pastor's wife Pam Sischo polled many of her friends in the ministry, asking them what tangible things speak love to them. Here are the results.

- Drop the pastor and his wife a note of encouragement. Don't just say, "Wonderful sermon!" Be specific. How did the sermon help you grow?
- Realize that your pastor is not a mind reader. Get the word to him if someone becomes ill or hospitalized or if there is a death in the family.
- Pastors and their families often don't have a lot of disposable income. Every once in a while, give them some "mad money" with which they may do whatever they wish.
- Offer to baby-sit for them for free so that they can have a night out alone occasionally.
- Don't buy into the old wives' tale that clergy and their families shouldn't be close friends with anyone at the church.

They are human too, and they need fellowship like the rest of us. Invite them over for dinner or an evening snack.

 av Often the pastor's wife or family ends up sitting alone in the pew. Sit with them.

av Surprise them with a day of free cleaning. Send them out to lunch while you do it.

av Let your pastor dream. Don't kill his vision with comments like "But we've never done it that way before" or "That just won't work."

av Take interest in their children. Don't expect them to be perfect. Offer to sit with them during the service to give the pastor's wife a needed break and to enable her to concentrate fully on her husband's sermon.

av Elizabeth Bruick writes, "When a new pastor was coming to our church, I made a sign-up chart for our Mom's Link Bible Study group. They could sign up for meals, groceries, fresh flowers or plants, and/or helping on the day of the move. On the day of their arrival we stocked their refrigerator and pantry with fresh food and staples and put fresh flowers and plants in their bathrooms and kitchen. It was very helpful for them not to have to worry about cooking or grocery shopping for the first few days!"

Come and Get It!

Here are a few tried-and-true make-ahead breakfast and dinner ideas that will help make your Sundays smoother.

Make-Ahead Breakfast Casserole
Contributed by Carmen Peterson

1 pound chopped ham
6 slices bread, cubed
8 eggs, slightly beaten
2 cups shredded sharp cheddar cheese
2 cups milk
salt and pepper to taste (we also like a pinch of
    basil or sage)

Combine eggs and milk. Fold in remaining ingredients. Place in a 9-by-13-inch pan that has been sprayed with cooking spray. Cover with plastic wrap and refrigerate overnight. In the morning, bake uncovered at 350 degrees for 45–50 minutes. Serve with fruit (cut up the night before) or juice. Serves 6.

Variations:

In place of the ham you may use any of the following:

- 1 lb. cooked crumbled bacon
- 1 lb. cooked ground sausage
- 1 lb cooked sausage links, sliced
- 2½ cups lightly sautéed mushrooms
- 2½ cups chopped cooked broccoli, drained
- 2½ cups cooked asparagus spears, chopped and well drained

Baked Oatmeal

The night before, combine the following in a large glass bowl. Cover and refrigerate.

3 cups old-fashioned oats (not quick oats)
½ cup melted butter
1 cup brown sugar
1½ teaspoons cinnamon
1½ cups buttermilk

In the morning, let mixture stand at room temperature for 5 minutes. Add:

2 beaten eggs
1½ teaspoons baking powder
½ teaspoon salt
¾ to 1 cup optional add-ins: chopped, peeled tart apples; raisins; nuts; chopped, peeled peaches; chopped bananas; chunky old-fashioned style peanut butter . . . anything goes!

Pour into a greased 9-by-9 pan. Bake for 35–45 minutes at 350 degrees. Cut into squares and place in a bowl. Top with milk or cream. Serves 8.

Slow Cooking Sunday Favorites

Leftovers from these Sunday dishes can be turned into Monday soups.

Lemon Herb Chicken

12 boneless, skinless chicken breasts
2 lemons, sliced
1 onion, sliced
2 teaspoons each of basil and oregano
1½ teaspoons lemon pepper
2 cloves of garlic, crushed (or 1 teaspoon dried, minced garlic)
½ teaspoon salt
½ cup lemon juice
¼ cup olive oil

Place chicken in Crock-Pot. Cover with lemons and onions. Pour juice and oil over and sprinkle on spices. Cook on high 4–6 hours. Serves 8–12.

To round out the meal, serve with any of the following:

- A rice side dish such as rice pilaf or wild rice blend
- Scalloped or augratin potatoes
- Glazed carrots. Simply steam a bag of baby carrots. Just before serving, toss with a few pats of butter, a sprinkle of ground cinnamon and a drizzle of pure maple syrup.
- A classic salad in the summer months such as potato salad, coleslaw, or macaroni salad
- Traditional green bean casserole

This next hearty soup idea is delicious served in bread bowls. You can purchase them at a local bakery.

Monday Soup Idea: Chicken Wild Rice Soup

½ cup butter (1 stick)

1 onion, chopped

1 cup chopped, peeled carrots

½ cup chopped celery

¾ cup flour

6 cups chicken stock (or 6 cups water with
  bouillon cubes to taste)

6-ounce package long grain and wild rice

2 cups leftover, chopped chicken

3 tablespoons cooking sherry (optional)

In a large soup kettle, melt butter and sauté onions, carrots, and celery until tender. Stir in flour. Gradually add stock until mixture comes to a boil, stirring constantly. Reduce heat to medium low. Prepare rice as directed on box, omitting oil and salt. Add rice and chicken to stock and simmer 10 minutes. Add sherry. Serves 10.

Variations:

Besides serving this thick soup in bread bowls, try pairing it with any of the following:

ᴥ Homemade buttermilk biscuits

ᴥ Refrigerated crescent rolls

ᴥ An assortment of whole grain crackers and chunks of cheese

ᴥ Homemade breadsticks. Just use your favorite pizza crust recipe, roll out on a greased cookie sheet and score with a knife before baking at 425° for 7–10 minutes. Upon removing from oven, brush with butter and sprinkle with Italian spices and parmesan cheese. Cut breadsticks along score markings.

A Life That Says Welcome

For this next Sunday menu idea, serve corn as a side dish. You'll be halfway to Monday supper!

Crock-Pot Ham with Mustard Sauce

In a Crock-Pot, layer 10–12 thick slices of fully cooked ham.

Pour over ham a mixture of:

> 20-ounce can crushed pineapple, drained
> ⅓ cup brown sugar
> dash of cinnamon

Cover and cook on low for 6 –8 hours or on high for 3–4. Serve with mustard sauce.

Grandma Shug's Mustard Sauce

My mother-in-law's famous sauce!

In a saucepan combine:

> 1 cup sugar
> 1 cup prepared mustard
> 1 can tomato soup
> ¾ cup vinegar
> 1 cup butter
> 4 eggs, well beaten

Cook over medium heat until it thickens, stirring constantly with a wire whisk. Cool and store in fridge. Can also be frozen. Delicious! (Also a hit for dipping chicken nuggets!)

Monday Soup Idea: Corn Chowder

In a large pot combine:

> 4 cups chicken stock (or 4 cups water with
> bouillon cubes to taste)
> 6 cups diced, peeled Yukon Gold potatoes
> 1 chopped onion
> ½ cup diced celery

Cook over medium heat for 30 minutes or until potatoes are tender. Then add:

> 3 tablespoons butter
> 1–2 cups finely chopped leftover ham
> 1½ cups leftover corn
> 2 cans cream of chicken soup
> 1½ cups sharp cheddar cheese

Just before serving, add:

> 8 ounces sour cream

Thin with a little milk if needed. Stir well. Serves 8–10.

Variations:

This can also be made with other leftover meats such as chopped, cooked chicken or turkey; cooked, crumbled bacon or leftover sliced sausage or bratwurst.

Italian Herbed Pot Roast

3–3½ pound English or sirloin tip roast, frozen
2 cups water
2 teaspoons dried, minced garlic
2 tablespoons beef bouillon
1 teaspoon marjoram
1 teaspoon oregano
1 tablespoon dried, minced onion
2 teaspoons basil
salt and pepper to taste

Place frozen roast in large roasting pan. Pour water over. Sprinkle with bouillon and seasonings. Cover and cook at 350 degrees for 3½ to 4 hours. Serves 6.

For side dishes, choose a few of the following:

- Large baked potatoes with all the fixins
- Redskin garlic mashed potatoes. Fill a crock pot with cubed redskin potatoes. Add 4–6 cups water. Cook on high 4–6 hours. Drain slightly and mash well adding milk, butter, and some chopped fresh garlic, if desired. If too dry, add more milk.
- Steamed broccoli, carrots, and red pepper chunks
- Homemade corn bread or biscuits served with honey
- Fried apples. Simply melt a few tablespoons of butter in a fry pan. Add peeled, sliced cooking apples and sauté lightly. Sprinkle with some cinnamon and brown sugar before serving.

Monday Soup Idea: Beef Vegetable Soup

In a large kettle combine:

> 12 cups beef stock (or 12 cups water with
> bouillon cubes to taste)
> 2 cups peeled, diced potatoes
> 1¼ cups sliced carrots
> 1 onion, chopped fine (¾ cup)
> 2 cups chopped cabbage
> 1 cup frozen peas
> 1 cup frozen corn
> 2 cups leftover chopped beef
> 14.5-ounce can diced tomatoes
> ¼ cup ketchup
> 2 tablespoons soy sauce
> 1 teaspoon dried, minced garlic (or one clove
> fresh, minced)
> 2 teaspoons basil
> 2 teaspoons oregano
> 2 bay leaves (optional)

Combine all and cook over medium heat for 30–45 minutes.
Then add:

> ¼ cup orzo, alphabet-shaped, or other small
> pasta or ¼ cup pearl barley

Cook 30–45 minutes longer, until pasta (or barley) is tender.
Remove bay leaves. Serves 8–10.

Awesome Cheesy Potatoes
Contributed by Mary Jo Thayer

The secret's in the slow roasting time.

6 large potatoes, cut into bite-sized chunks
2 large onions, coarsely chopped
1½ cups shredded cheddar cheese
½ cup butter, cut up
2 teaspoons salt
1 teaspoon ground black pepper
1 teaspoon ground red pepper
2 teaspoons garlic powder
4 tablespoons water

Mix all ingredients together in a roasting pan and cover. Roast in a 325 degree oven for 1½ to 2 hours (stirring every 20 minutes) or until potatoes are nice and soft. Or wrap potatoes well in heavy foil and grill, turning package every 20 minutes. Potatoes can take up to 2½ hours, depending on the grill temperature. May be made a day ahead and then reheated. Serves 6–8.

These potatoes accompany the following main dishes beautifully:

- Steaks on the grill
- Baked chicken or roast turkey
- Pork chops and gravy
- Traditional pot roast
- Hamburgers and hot dogs, picnic style
- Baked honey glazed ham

Boston Grahams

This is my friend Debi Davis's recipe and an easy make-ahead Sunday dessert.

2 small packages vanilla instant pudding
3 squares unsweetened baking chocolate
3½ cups milk
¼ cup water
8 ounces Cool Whip, thawed
3 tablespoons butter
45 graham cracker squares
1 teaspoon vanilla
2 tablespoons light corn syrup
4 cups powdered sugar

Mix pudding and milk with blender until thickened. Gently fold in Cool Whip. Place 15 crackers in a 9-by-13-inch pan in three rows of five. Cover with half the pudding mixture. Layer 15 more crackers, then the rest of pudding. End with remaining 15 crackers. In a saucepan, melt over low heat the remaining ingredients except vanilla and sugar. Remove from heat. Add vanilla and enough sugar to make a smooth, fairly thick frosting. Keep stirring hard—it will come! Pour immediately over top of dessert in pan and then seal with foil. Refrigerate at least 24 hours. Serves 12–15.

Peanut Butter–Apple Crunch

½ cup smooth peanut butter
½ cup butter, softened
½ cup rolled oats
½ cup flour
1½ cups brown sugar
¼ teaspoon salt

A Life That Says Welcome

8–10 large, tart cooking apples (Granny Smith,
    Cortland, Spy, Yellow Delicious, etc.)
1 tablespoon lemon juice
⅔ cup sugar
¼ cup flour

With a pastry blender in a medium bowl, blend first six
ingredients until smooth. Peel and slice apples and place in a
greased 9-by-13-inch pan. Sprinkle lemon juice, sugar, flour,
and water over apples. Top with peanut butter/oats mixture.
Bake at 375 degrees until apples are tender, about 40 minutes.
Serve plain or with ice cream or whipped cream for the deluxe
version! Serves 8–10.

Hot Fudge Ice Cream Cake

1 cup flour
3 tablespoons olive oil
¾ cup sugar
1½ teaspoons vanilla extract
2 tablespoons cocoa powder
1¼ cups packed brown sugar
1½ teaspoons baking powder
¼ cup cocoa powder
½ cup milk
1¾ cups boiling water

In an ungreased 9-inch-square metal pan, combine all but
brown sugar, ¼ cup cocoa, and boiling water. Mix well. (At
this point, pan can be sealed with foil and refrigerated until
later if desired.) Then sprinkle on brown sugar and cocoa.
Pour boiling water over the top. Bake uncovered at 350
degrees for 40 minutes. Remove and cool slightly. Serve with
ice cream. Serves 6.

❧ 9 ❧

Hospitality on the Road

Is hospitality limited only to your home? If we are unable for some reason or season to open our home to others, are we exempt from offering hospitality?

I think not.

I am convinced that God wants to grow us in the area of hospitality whether or not we are able to use our home. After all, kindness knows no limits, welcome has no bounds. We can seek to be the kind of Christian who makes others feel comfortable, loved, and wanted simply by being with them.

I have known many such people. And I admit to you that being this type of person doesn't always come naturally for me. I am just as prone to being self-centered, demanding, and high-maintenance as the next gal. What has inspired me to swim against that natural tide has been the wonderful examples God has set before me. They are those of whom I can honestly say, "When I grow up, I want to be just like them!"

My best friend from college is just such a person. You will long for a friend such as her as I tell you about her. But I found her first!

Kelly Hovermale and I became fast friends nearly twenty-five years ago when we were placed on the same floor during our freshman year at Spring Arbor University. I hailed from the large nearby capital city. She was from a faraway, tiny, one-horse town. I was the youngest child in my family. She was the oldest. I had only a brother. She had only sisters. I was outgoing and loud. She was reserved and quiet. If you ever needed proof that opposites attract, we were it. She calmed me down; I livened her up a bit. She got me to think before I acted; I taught her to jump in feet first.

For nearly three years we shared joys and heartaches, never living more than a few hundred feet apart. She was rarely too busy to let me drop in to her dorm room for a chat. (I did most of the chatting; she did the listening.) She sent me encouraging notes in the campus mail. She saved me a seat in chapel and in the dining hall. When she said she would pray for me, I knew the Lord would be hearing from her many times in the near future with my name ever on her lips. She cared about my family, my future, and my dreams.

Then, during our junior year, she left to marry her Mr. Wonderful, my friend Greg, on the third weekend in June. I caught the bouquet at their wedding. Todd caught the—well, he was pushed forward and forced to pick up the garter! (We were already nearly engaged. No other guy would dare touch it.) On the third weekend in June the following year, Todd and I tied the knot as well. And yes, Kelly and I were each other's bridesmaids.

Even though I only lived in the dormitory with her for two and a half years, we have remained close friends for two and a half decades. Kelly continues to be one of the most welcoming people in my life.

For the past twenty-one years we have lived hours apart, but she has remained close to my heart. As the times have changed, she has been there to encourage me as a wife, a mom, a writer, and a speaker. She knows when my somewhat scared son has a dental appointment and when my daughter will be traveling with the youth group for the weekend. She knows where I'm speaking and at what time, even if I am in a different time zone. And she takes these requests before the throne of God.

She often uses the U.S. mail to deliver her kindness: a delicate hand-sewn treasure; a rich, homespun woolen ware; a handwritten recipe she thinks my family will enjoy; clipped coupons for items she knows that I buy; a bookmark imprinted with Scripture that speaks uncannily to my soul; a single bag of my favorite tea.

Kelly is an example of someone who does not confine her hospitality to within her four walls. She is welcoming wherever she happens to be, and she uses her God-given skills and personality to offer refreshment to me and speak truth over my life.

And she isn't the only treasure God has given me. Take my "ladies," as my husband fondly calls them.

Each year I am a featured speaker at the Hearts at Home National Conference in Bloomington, Illinois. I began doing this several years ago, before I ever wrote a book or appeared on a national radio or television show. I was just a mom leading a workshop. (And really, that is how I still see myself!) After one of my talks, three women approached me. Teena, Lesa, and Cyndi smiled as they sweetly told me that I was their favorite speaker of the weekend. I was honored and, truthfully, shocked and surprised. I thanked them for their kind words, and before they left, they had another attendee snap a picture of the four of us for their scrapbooks. I still smile when I think about it. Little did they know the insecurity I felt speaking at a national conference for the first time alongside a bunch of top-notch, well-known, "real" speakers, which I feared I was not. They made me feel so wanted and at home.

Each year since then, the same scenario plays. These sweet gals attend that conference as an annual mommy getaway. And sometime during the day, they find me, now usually at my book table. Again someone is solicited to snap another picture. And now that I appear on the main stage in the keynote session performing drama or serving as emcee, they sit near the front, smile heartily, and wave like crazy. They are *my* ladies, and I love 'em!

When I need an idea for a project I am working on, these gals are among the first to respond. When my father-in-law died last spring, they sent a beautiful bouquet to the funeral home, even though they live a state away and have never met anyone in my husband's family. These gals are pictures of love and support. They are wonderfully hospitable. And I have never even stepped foot in any of their homes.

I think modern Christendom would do well to have more such people in its ranks—people who look for the best in others and, as a result, bring it out in themselves. So often our churches are filled with Christian sibling squabbles, our pews with constant complaints. We are adept at pointing out what is wrong with the program, the service, the building, or the staff. I know. I've done my fair share of pointing! Imagine instead if we really took to heart the biblical admonition to honor and give preference to one another instead (Rom. 12:9–11).

Finding Your Niche

Perhaps you also want to be someone who blesses others with her talents and time. But where to begin? At the beginning, of course.

Think back over your life for a moment. What qualities and talents have others noticed in you even from the very beginning

---

A Life That Says Welcome

of your childhood? Are you skilled at working with your hands or decorating? Have you, unlike me, always been keen in the kitchen? Can you write poetry? Or paint? Do children just adore being around you?

Some of the earliest feedback I received from teachers, family members, and friends seemed to follow a pattern. The three things I heard most often were "Karen is a great writer," "This child is so overly dramatic," and "*Man*, can that girl talk!" And you know what? These are exactly the areas where God is choosing to use me. I write both books and magazine articles. I am the director of drama for Hearts at Home, and each year I get to perform skits and recite monologues in front of over ten thousand moms. And yes, I can talk. I even get paid to do it!

But before God used me outside of my four walls, he tested me in the realm of my family. I spent several hidden years at home rocking babies while I spoke and told tales, acting out Bible stories during family devotions and writing love letters to my husband and prose pieces for my family's eyes only. Then God gave me permission and privilege to use these gifts elsewhere.

Now I have an assignment for you. Make a list of your own talents and abilities. Don't be shy or feel that somehow you are not being humble. I used to think that being humble meant you hung your head and never took a compliment gracefully but instead, when told you were skilled in a particular area, you insisted, "Oh, I am not."

I now know being humble means having an accurate assessment of yourself. Not thinking more highly of yourself than you ought, but giving a fair estimation of the areas God has gifted you in and those he has not.

Next begin to brainstorm ways you can use your talents, abilities, and trades to bless others in your life, beginning with your family members. Don't let your skills sit on a shelf, so to speak. Dust them off and use them! Others of us need them in the body of Christ, and precious yet-to-be-believers will be drawn to the Lord through them as well. I have seen it happen time and time again with my daughter's Sunday school teacher Diana's homemade bread, my friend Trish's talent for sewing and crafts, and my accountability partner Mary's special gift of intercessory prayer.

You may want to consult a family member or close friend in order to get their input during this process. Sometimes others see in us what we cannot see in ourselves. Ask them where they feel your talents, skills, and special personality traits lie. What are some ways you can use these to bless and encourage others?

Those who are proficient in practicing this "hospitality on the road" have a knack for making others feel at ease even in unfamiliar territory. This week as I write, my two oldest are off at church camp in the upper part of Michigan's lower peninsula. The staff at Camp Barakel make the children feel welcome from the minute their feet touch down on their woodsy soil. Campers are greeted warmly and personally by the counselors and staff. Careful attention is given to detail. The cabins are clean and inviting, however rustic they may be. Every meal is homemade and delicious. The staff sport genuine smiles that accurately reflect the love of the Lord. The speakers and song leaders are top-notch not only in skill but in their authentic concern for the souls of these kids.

All of this combines to make for a wonderful experience for these kids, many of them who are away from home overnight for the very first time. My friend Debi volunteers in the camp kitchen for one week each summer when her kids themselves are campers. Debi is definitely a gal who takes her hospitality on the road. Whenever she encounters a child from our church, whether in the food line or out on the grounds, they are met with a smile, a hug, and a quick check of sunscreen. She's even been known to sneak them an extra cookie at mealtimes. (Shhh!) So many moms at our church find out what week Debi will be serving as cook before they sign their children up for camp. They know she will offer welcome and warmth to their loved one while they are three long hours from home.

Where else do we witness the practice of "hospitality on the road"? Everywhere! Think of the smiling store greeter, the caring volunteer at the surgery waiting room desk, the cheerful room mother, the faithful Sunday school teacher, and on and on and on! These people are perfectly positioned to offer welcome on the road on a regular basis.

But where can you and your family begin to practice hospitality on the road? The possibilities are endless. First, just take a look at your typical week. Nothing out of the norm, just an average week in the life of your family. Where do you go? Who do you see? With whom does your life naturally intersect?

In the course of a week our family sees dozens of people. The mail lady, the grocery store clerk, the Wal-Mart worker, our church staff, several neighbors, a few teachers at the home-school academy, a widow whose cat we sometimes feed when she's gone, the UPS man, my sons' baseball coaches, the gas station attendant—and the list goes on. Do we need to think of something special to do for each of these people every week? Of course not. But we can remember that they have been placed by God in our lives for a reason and made for a purpose. We can certainly be sensitive to the Lord's leading, recognizing that small nudge that prompts us to say or give something of kindness to them.

We can also offer welcome on the road to society's forgotten. If you have never taken your family to serve at a soup kitchen or homeless shelter, please set up a time to do it. We have had the honor to occasionally serve at a few different rescue missions and soup kitchens. You don't need to give a parental lecture on poverty and privilege. The experience speaks for itself. Children will learn to love the less-than-lovely as they serve them a hot meal or pass out personal supplies. Don't wait until they are older. We went for the first time when our oldest was just three. She was assigned the task of passing out olives and pickles with a welcoming smile. Her heart was touched as she saw children her own age whose only hot meal was the one they received at the soup kitchen each noon. Contact abuse shelters or local orphanages as well. They may be delighted to put your family to work as you seek to bring sunshine into the lives of those less fortunate than you.

If you look closely around you, it won't take long for you to figure out ways you and your family can be a blessing without necessarily involving your home.

Commit to striving to be a person of welcome, making others feel at home with you wherever they are. Help them weather the storms of life by your encouraging words both spoken and written and your prayers uttered on their behalf. And take whatever gifts, abilities, and talents God has given you, and don't you dare hide them under a bushel. NO! Use them to minister to those with whom your life path logically crosses.

But keep this in mind: as always, check your motives. Matthew 5:16 says, "Let your light shine before men, that they may see your good deeds and praise your Father in heaven." We want to point others to him, not to take the credit ourselves. We want to be a mirror accurately reflecting the face of our Father, causing others to be drawn to the beautiful light.

∽Welcome Ideas∾

Take Your Show on the Road

My mom was the original hospitality-on-the-road gal. She always came up with such clever ideas to bless her family and friends. Her life served as an inspiration to me. Now, here are some examples to help you get started taking your show on the road. I'm sure you can think of many more!

1. When you are a guest in someone's home, take along a little hostess gift. A candle, a flower, or a jar of homemade jam or preserves is a kind way to say thank you.
2. Take a pretty tea set to the home of a shut-in or elderly friend. Serve tea and muffins and enjoy a leisurely visit.
3. Show up at the home of someone in need of your service. Rake their leaves, shovel their driveway and sidewalk, weed their flower bed, or wash their windows. Bring a snack along to share with them when the work is done.
4. Encourage the fellow soccer moms and dads on the side lines at a game or practice. Take a thermos of hot cider and some fresh donuts to have while you watch your kids play.
5. Bless those in your local government by taking a platter of cookies and brownies to the local school board or city council meeting.
6. Mail a "five-dollar date night." Send an anniversary card with a five-dollar bill tucked in. Include a list of questions on some pretty paper. These are designed to initiate conversation on their five-dollar date. List questions like: "Tell about the first time you noticed or met each other. What details can you remember?" or "What would be your idea

of the perfect getaway weekend just for the two of you?" or "Tell each other the five things you most appreciate about the other's personality." They then take the questions and the five dollars and go on a date for coffee, lemonade, or an ice cream cone to discuss their questions.

7. For a friend who has moved away, send a handwritten letter along with a pack of forget-me-not seeds. When they bloom each year, your friend will remember you.

8. Think about other places where someone new comes on board—the PTA, the Little League team, at church. Think of a way to welcome them and make them feel at home.

9. At Easter time one year, our family loaded the kids in a red wagon, strolled up and down the streets of our neighborhood, and passed out copies of the *Jesus* film by Campus Crusade along with some bags of microwave popcorn. We heard back from many of these folks, and they loved getting a gift that portrayed the real meaning of Easter.

10. When going to the doctor, dentist, or hairdresser, take along a home-baked treat and a simple note thanking them for their service to you throughout the year.

11. Know a new mom with a baby? Sure, take her a meal, but take along your cleaning bucket too. Clean her house while she and the baby nap. Or tote with you an empty laundry basket. Kidnap her dirty laundry and take it home with you. Wash, dry, and fold it and return a few hours later with her now clean clothes.

12. Moving and setting up house can be a stressful time. Think of ways to lighten the load of those in such a situation. When we moved into our home, my friend Dorothy offered us some hospitality on the road. She showed up with her paints, stencils, and stenciling brush and helped us to work on a few rooms. She also brought a pot of soup,

A Life That Says Welcome

some bread, and ice cream sandwiches for us to enjoy as we took a break.

13. Use the U.S. mail to deliver your greetings. Send a care package to a college student, a camper, or a faraway relative. You can even make a movie night in a box. Include microwave popcorn and old-fashioned movie house candies like Junior Mints or Sugar Babies. Tuck in a home movie of your kids for grandma and grandpa or a gift certificate for a movie rental for that college student. My friend Lesa Bruns has this idea for blessing college students: "A wonderful gift for someone who is going off to college is to give them an 'order form' made by you along with a stamped envelope addressed to you. On this 'order form' put things like 'My favorite cookie is: _____. I really crave: _____. A snack I would love is: _____. One item I really need is: _____' etc. They can fill in the blanks, send it back to you, and then you have a list of things that you can put together in a care package to send to them. Some items I have found handy to include are postage stamps, note cards, batteries, and pizza coupons."

14. Lesa offers another idea: "We have a friend who just recently finished all of her scheduled rounds of chemotherapy for breast cancer, and we had a party! All of those who are close friends of hers and had helped support her with meals and childcare, errands, etc., all got together for a pitch-in meal to celebrate with her this milestone!"

15. If a new neighbor is building a home near you, Lesa suggests taking pictures as the house progresses and then surprising them with a small album/scrapbook and baked good as you welcome them into the neighborhood.

16. Sue Smith offers this creative idea: "We adopt older people in the neighborhood as a tool to teach the kids to honor and respect the elderly. One couple experienced the sor-

row of the husband's death, so we started to invite the widow for dinner and dropped by with fresh-picked produce or conversation. One summer day, I decided the kids needed to walk off a little energy, so we headed for the widow's house. I was stopped by my four-year-old, who wanted to take cut roses to her from our flower bed. I was disgruntled—one more delay. I did go back in the house for a pair of scissors to cut all the best roses for the neighbor, though. She didn't say much when she received them. However, a week later the widow stopped by our house. She told us that her wedding anniversary was on the day of our last visit and our roses were the only flowers she received for the day. The day we visited she was moved by the gift of flowers and couldn't express her gratitude without many tears. It just goes to show that the Holy Spirit speaks through our children. I learned that we parents need to listen and take heed more often. This past Christmas, we invited her for supper. The kids were memorizing the Christmas story from one of their children's Bibles, and they put on a 'theater performance' with admission tickets, cardboard characters, and blankets. They made a huge mess in the living area, but this widow was so blessed by their creativity and message that the memory kept her company during her sleepless night. The next day she told her Bible study ladies all about the spontaneous performance. We even invite her to join us for bedtime prayers if she is still around for 'tucking in.' It has been touching for her to experience a family today passing on the faith."

17. Cynthia Bontrager gives this idea: "On three separate occasions, people I know and love have been attending to their loved one in the hospital for extended periods of time. Because I have had small children during these times and

couldn't always visit as often as I would have liked, I decided to create a basket full of 'love, prayers, and sustenance.' In this basket I put notes of encouragement and cards with Bible verses and specific prayers for their loved one and packed it full of homemade goodies and other much appreciated nonperishable surprises such as mints, gum, crackers and peanut butter, juice, single servings of applesauce, pudding, or other things quick and easy to grab yet easy on the stomach. Items in this basket were mainly consumed by the family of the ill person as they used it to sustain them when they didn't want to leave the room to go get something to eat. However, this basket also contained a favorite treat for the ill person, something they were able and allowed to eat, something that sounded extra good to them. This basket, if applicable, also contained 'childcare coupons' that the family could 'cash in' during one of the many trips made to the hospital. This made it easier for them to ask me to help with their children; they just used a coupon!"

Heartfelt Holidays

At the holidays, seek to practice seemingly random but purposefully planned acts of kindness. Here are some ideas for blessing others during the holiday hustle and bustle:

- Bake cookies for the break room at the local discount store on the day after Thanksgiving when the store is swamped. Leave a thank-you note praising the employees' hard work around the holidays. What a sharp contrast to the fifty customers they encountered earlier in the day screaming because they ran out of the latest electronic gadget that was advertised!

- Take hot cocoa to the department store bell-ringers in town.
- Scrape windshields in the grocery store parking lot on a snowy day. Leave a little note that reads, "Random acts of kindness. Pass it on."
- Hang a thermos of hot cider on the mailbox for the mail carrier.
- My kids' favorite—leave a plate of freshly baked brownies out for the garbage men!
- Think of those who have recently lost a loved one and are facing their first Christmas alone. Include them in your family's activities or take a dinner to them one night and help them decorate their home.
- Remember those who must work on the holidays in the hospital or at the police or fire station. Take them a platter of fresh vegetables and dip or assorted cheeses and crackers. Include some artwork crafted by your children depicting them in their various roles.
- Adopt a Christmas family. Contact a local agency to get the name and address of a needy family. If possible, choose one that has children near the same age as yours. Shop for clothing, food, and toys for them. Deliver your items as a family. Try to keep in touch with them throughout the year with an occasional note or card.

∞ 10 ∞

Practice Makes Perfect

"If at first you don't succeed, try, try again." "Good, better, best, never let it rest until the good is better and the better is best." "Practice makes perfect."

Okay, so in the area of hospitality, practice won't make us perfect, but it will sure make us more prepared. That is what we'll focus on now: tips and ideas designed to help us get into the hospitality routine, to be primed and ready for whomever God will bring our way.

First, before we pick up a broom or turn on the oven, we must ready our hearts. We must be willing to expect the unexpected. Plan on it. It's a nonnegotiable. Every so often, when God feels you are ready (or have something to learn in this area), he will bring someone along who will need a bed for the night, a nourishing hot meal, or even just a cup of cool water. How will you react? Will you fuss and fume? Will you apologize and fumble? Or will you say, "Come on in, I was expecting you!" (Well, sort of!) Don't tell me you simply are not an organized soul. Being organized mostly boils down to being prepared. We can all do things to prepare. When we anticipate these visitors in advance, their arrival won't throw us for such a big loop. Expect the unexpected and then accept them as well.

Oh, I wish this came naturally to me! I admit that I still wrestle with so much in this area. I am not innately wired to welcome without worry (though I will give you a peek into the lives of many who are). I can still fret and stress about scores of things. When the doorbell rings and unexpected company comes, my concerns commence. I wish the house were cleaner. I wonder what the bathroom looks like. I trouble over the food I might need to prepare. And mostly I whine about the loss of my time. What about what *I* had planned to do? Even while trying to get the words of this manuscript out of my brain and into my computer, many times my attitude was tested. Once a friend of ours who lost his wife to cancer a few years back wanted me to keep his four-year-old son for the weekend so he could attend an out-of-town wedding for a few days. My initial response was "I can't take in another child for three days. Don't you know I'm busy writing a book on hospitality, for Pete's sake!" No sooner had the words formed in my mind than I saw the irony (and shame!) of that mind-set.

Yes, I watched his child. Our whole family had a wonderful weekend with this dear little one. I trusted that God would give me the time to write later, and he did. As I need to remind myself often, people are more important than projects.

I need to learn to keep a quiet heart. To trust that if God has allowed an interruption in my day, it serves a purpose. To believe that the time to finish what work I thought needed to be done will be given. To accept that he is diverting me from my "plan A" to his greater plan.

Back to the Basics

For now, we will focus on a few things, starting with ideas for what to feed your visitors and what to do while they are there. Here you will also meet a number of people who are known for their hospitality. I hope the tributes that were written about them will serve as inspiration as you strive to be hospitable, no matter how new you may be to this whole notion. We'll also tackle overnight company.

I am including below an interview with my sister-in-love Erin, who for many years ran a wildly successful bed-and-breakfast. While I know we aren't trying to run an award-winning inn, we can learn tips from those who make their living offering welcome to overnight guests throughout the year.

An Interview with an Innkeeper

My husband's sister Erin and her husband, Bo, were the proprietors of The Mango Inn, a lovely bed-and-breakfast in Lake Worth in Palm Beach County, Florida. They purchased three run-down buildings on the property and transformed them into a beautiful getaway for travelers. They became well known for not only the exquisite décor but also their fine cuisine. Some of Erin's recipes were featured in culinary magazines including *Southern Living*.

With such an expert right in my own family, I decided to interview Erin about what was important in running a successful and welcoming bed-and-breakfast. Her answers can provide us with ideas and motivation as we too seek to make others feel welcome when staying in our homes.

What are the most important aspects of running a bed-and-breakfast that ensure that your guests feel welcome and refreshed and will desire to stay at your B&B again?

- Serve an unforgettable breakfast.

- Have the highest quality mattresses and linens, plump *real* down pillows (not feather—there is a difference!), and synthetic pillows as an alternative for those who have allergies.

- Make your guests feel like your home/inn is "their" home to enjoy while they stay, and don't make them feel like they are an intruder or imposing.

- Don't overlook the smallest detail—from monogrammed bed linens to fresh flowers in the room, magazines for both sexes, bottled water—things that say "I thought of you" before your guest arrives.

- Anticipate every possible need they may have—robes, slippers, iron and ironing board, and amenities of body lotion, shampoo, conditioner, hair cap, hair dryer, mending kit. Have available personal items such as disposable razors, toothbrushes, toothpaste, and feminine products for the guest who may have forgotten such things or whose luggage was lost en route.

- Create an ambience of romance and relaxation. People go to inns to get away from their hectic lives. Everything should encourage peacefulness. Soft music at the pool, quiet places for contemplation on the grounds where people can sit and read or listen to the trees rustle in the breeze and share the day with one another.

What advice do you have about food? Does it need to be gourmet? Regional? Colorful? Simple, but plenty of it?
    All of the above. Travelers expect an excellent and generous breakfast when they go to a B&B. Gourmet doesn't have to be complicated and fussy. When you are utilizing fresh, seasonal products, you are providing the best that is available to your guests. Most people are very visual, so presentation is very important, and garnishes are the "ribbon" on the gift, so to speak.

They should be colorful and fresh too. A kaleidoscope of color is visually pleasing and easily attainable through the selection of your garnish to complement your food.

Do you have any advice on décor? How can you make rooms functional and beautiful too?

It can be challenging at times to make a room functional and beautiful too. But you have to remember that it's always about the guest and their comfort, not about displaying all those cute knickknacks you've been collecting for the past ten years. It's about having space for them to put their things while they are with you. Have comfortable furniture that can be used and not just looked at, candles for mood, and lots of magazines for every taste so people will sit a spell and enjoy the tranquility.

Keeping things simple is often best unless you have a real eye for putting clutter together and not making it feel like clutter. Using colors that are in the same family is often easiest for novices. But you should always have that little "surprise" accent or accessory that people would not expect. It gives a room its own personality.

How can you personally make your guests feel at home through your attitude, conversation, and demeanor?

Always smile and *really* listen to them. Having an inn is about human interaction and relationships, unlike staying in a hotel where there in little personal interaction with staff and certainly not with the owner. Accommodate their requests if at all possible, because the guest is always right. You want them to leave feeling like there was nothing they needed and couldn't have. That's what will bring them back or at the very least make them tell their friends about your inn.

What are some things NOT to do when having guests into your home?

Never let guests feel like they are intruding. You have invited them into your home as a guest. So when the kids are late getting ready to leave for their after-school activities and your temper is short, or you're two hours behind on your chores because you've been "entertaining," or the cookies burn in the oven, don't ever let your guest feel like if they weren't there, these things wouldn't be happening and you wouldn't feel stressed.

Thanks to Erin for her expert advice!

Drop-Ins

Because I live in town and many of my friends are country gals, I tend to get more "drop-in" guests than most. When I first quit work to be home with Mackenzie, I let many of my friends know that if they were ever in town and wanted to drop by or have me watch their kids while they ran errands, I would be available to do so. I lived only a few short blocks from our town's shopping district where a grocery store, drugstore, and department store were located. When I had small preschool-aged children, my days were most often spent at home and usually were arranged around my kids' naptimes. Having drop-in company seemed to fit well with me, and I was happy to watch an extra toddler or two so a friend could shop alone and in less time.

As my family has grown and my kids have gotten older, the drop-in company we have has changed a bit. Now it often is a preteen sibling whose older sister is taking a driver's ed class. She'd rather come to our house while Mom runs errands until the class time is through. Sometimes I have friends who pop in simply because they want to talk or they are upset about something. I've also had crisis situations where someone's car broke down in town or they needed to rush a child to the hospital, leaving the other children in my care. I even took in my friend's three children on the spur of the moment the day she found out her husband was having an affair.

A Life That Says Welcome

I wish I could tell you I've always had a willing and cheerful attitude when these situations arose, but I'd be lying. Oftentimes I do. At other times, at the least I have felt uneasy when I sensed a guest wanted me to stop what I was doing and visit. Often what I was doing needed to be done on a schedule or by a certain deadline. Instead of simply telling her so, I would secretly stew and plot how I could get her out of my home. Sometimes I've even felt taken advantage of by a friend who nearly wore out her welcome, in my estimation, expecting me to drop what I was doing and watch her kids at the drops of many hats!

I am still learning in this area, but here are some tips I have learned that can help you deal with unexpected guests.

- Have an open-door policy, but define what that is. Say something like, "If you are ever in town and would like to drop in for a visit or have me watch your child while you get caught up on errands, give me a quick call on your cell phone. If I can clear my schedule at that point, I'd love to see you or help you out. If I'm unable to, we'll set a date to get together in the near future."

- When a friend pops in and you are going about your daily routine and not under any tight deadline, drop what you are doing for a few minutes and at the very least offer her something to drink. After a short while say something like, "I'm glad you stopped in, and feel free to stay for a while. I'll bring my laundry in here so I can continue to fold it while we visit." If she offers to help, let her. By all means, if the laundry or dishes can wait, then let them! But be sensitive to what your hubby would want. If he'd be less than thrilled to find out that you let the house go or forgot to pay the pile of bills while you chatted all day with a friend, then work while you chat. Remember, family first!

Practice Makes Perfect

❧ Let her know how much time you can take out of your daily routine. "I'm so glad you're here! I have a half hour before I need to start supper. We can sneak in a good visit until then." Then, unless her situation warrants more time, stick to your plan.

❧ Let children know rules and boundaries. Be polite, but if there are items that are off-limits to your own children, then by all means, don't let another mom's child carry around the heirloom glass item. Been there, broke that.

❧ Many moms in my survey said it was the little touches that mattered most. Offer your guest ice water with a slice of lemon or sprig of fresh mint; fix them a cup of tea or hot cider or even instant cappuccino. Make sure their children are involved in doing something fun. If they are having a rough day, bring them a throw or quilt to cuddle up in or some tissues and an emergency dose of chocolate.

❧ Be sensitive to God's Spirit leading you. If your friend's needs are great, he'll give you a gentle nudge letting you know that this visit is more than a casual one. Trust that the interruption is part of his plan for your life that day. Don't grumble. It doesn't help. Instead, keep a quiet heart.

Overnight Guests

Although we've never had company live with us for an extended period of time, we have had our fair share of overnight guests. Todd's parents have always lived nearly three hours from us and have come to stay several times a year. We have missionary friends and college buddies who also spend the night with us. And then there are our kids' friends! Each month of the year finds us hosting an assortment of sleepy-eyed teenage girls or bright-eyed and bushy-tailed boys up at the crack of dawn ready to go pester squirrels with their BB guns. Yep, hospitality means sometimes guests spend the night. Here are some dos and don'ts to remember when hosting overnight callers:

- Decide where they will keep their things, even if there isn't space in the room where they will sleep. Show them the spot and make sure others respect their personal space and property.
- Have a pleasant place for them to lay their head for the night. It doesn't have to be a real guest bedroom. At our old house, company slept on a hand-me-down pull-out sofa we had in our unfinished basement. We purchased a new slipcover for it and made sure it was outfitted with warm, flannel sheets as the room was sometimes chilly. We found a dresser at a yard sale that they could use to put their things in. We painted the walls white to lighten the room and would set out a bouquet of fresh flowers or leave chocolates on their pillows like a real inn would.
- Stock their room with needed items. A lamp for evening reading, a mirror for getting ready, and a working alarm clock are the basics.
- Show them the bathroom. Have a space cleared on the counter or in a cabinet for them to place their toiletries. Roll a few wash cloths and tie with a ribbon. Place them on top of the bath towel they will use. Fill a small basket with other items they might possibly need: soap, shampoo, toothpaste, toothbrush, lotion, etc. Look for these items in special scents and trial sizes. Or if a hotel says you can take them, then by all means, bring them home!
- Let them know the laundry facilities are available to them. Check each day to see if they need anything washed and dried or ironed.

- Have a pitcher of water and glasses in their room. Have the refrigerator well stocked with juices, spritzers, or teas for them to enjoy if they are thirsty.
- Consider placing a basket of fruit or shortbread cookies and chocolates in their room. Tailor it to their liking. Include anything that says, "Welcome! We were thinking of you!"
- If a coffee lover will be staying with you and you don't drink coffee, consider purchasing a small coffeemaker that they can use in their room.
- Let them know your schedule and be aware of theirs. Discuss breakfast the night before. Let them know when supper will be served and make sure it works in their schedule.
- Before they come, discuss dietary restrictions.
- Pet- and child-proof your guests' room. They will appreciate the protection it will provide their belongings. Also, before arrival, find out if your guests have pet allergies. Rid your place of pet hair and try to keep your animal away from them as much as you can.
- Let them know if there are any quirks to how things work at your house. Does the hot water take a while to run? Does the front door lock need a little push to the right in order to open?
- If you can't always be home when they will be returning, give them a spare house key.
- Treat them like both guests and part of the family. People feel uneasy if you seem to be begrudgingly putting life on hold just to entertain them. As a rule, go about your daily routine, but make them a part of it.

Recipes for Your Bed-and-Breakfast

I just couldn't write a book on hospitality without providing a few of my sister-in-law's wonderful recipes from her bed-and-breakfast. Some of her spectacular Mango Inn recipes have been featured in *Southern Living* magazine. Here she shares a few of her favorite recipes with you!

This recipe is made the night before and then refrigerated until ready to bake. A fall favorite!

Baked Apple French Toast with Spicy Cider Syrup

 1 cup brown sugar
 ½ cup butter
 2 tablespoons corn syrup
 2 tart apples, peeled and sliced
 1 loaf day-old French bread
 5 eggs
 1½ cups milk
 1½ teaspoons vanilla

Spicy Cider Syrup

1 cup sugar
3 tablespoons all-purpose flour
¼ teaspoon cinnamon
¼ teaspoon nutmeg
2 cups apple cider
2 tablespoons lemon juice
¼ cup butter

In microwave-safe bowl, combine brown sugar, butter, and corn syrup; cover with paper towel. Microwave on high power until butter is melted. Whisk together into a thick syrup. Pour into 9-by-13-inch glass baking dish. Arrange apple slices over mixture. Slice bread into ¾-inch slices. Place on top of apples. Whisk together in small bowl eggs, milk, and vanilla. Pour over bread. Cover with plastic wrap and refrigerate overnight.

In the morning, bake uncovered at 350 degrees for 40 minutes. While baking, prepare syrup by combining sugar, flour, and spices in a 2-quart saucepan. Stir in cider and lemon juice. Cook over medium heat, stirring constantly until mixture thickens and boils. Boil and stir one minute. Remove from heat. Stir in butter. Serve over baked French toast. Serves 6–8.

A Life That Says Welcome

Blueberry Gingerbread Pancakes

A new twist on an old favorite.

> 2 cups unbleached flour
> 1½ teaspoons baking powder
> 1¼ teaspoons ground ginger
> ¾ teaspoon pumpkin pie spice
> ¼ teaspoon baking soda
> ¼ teaspoon salt
> ¾ cup mild (light) molasses
> ¾ cup buttermilk
> 2 large eggs
> 3 tablespoons vegetable oil
> 2 cups blueberries (fresh are best, but frozen
>   work too)
> additional vegetable oil

Sift dry ingredients into medium bowl. Whisk molasses, buttermilk, eggs, and 3 tablespoons oil in large bowl to blend. Add dry ingredients and whisk just until smooth. Fold in blueberries.

Heat large nonstick skillet or griddle over medium-low heat. Brush with oil. Drop 3 tablespoons batter for each pancake. Using back of spoon, spread each pancake to 3-inch round. Cook until bottoms are lightly golden, about 1½ minutes. Flip and cook until heated through. If desired, transfer pancakes to a preheated 200-degree oven to keep warm until serving. Re-oil skillet between batches. Serve with real butter and maple syrup.

Here's a hearty, no-fail breakfast idea.

Santa Fe Strata

1 pound ground sausage
1 6-ounce can tomatoes and chiles with juices
9 large eggs
¾ cup flour
2 teaspoons baking powder
½ teaspoon salt
1 teaspoon chopped fresh garlic (or ½ teaspoon
    dried minced garlic)
2 cups frozen corn, thawed
12 ounces sour cream
12 ounces cottage cheese
1½ cups sharp cheddar cheese
1½ cups Romano cheese

In a skillet, brown sausage. Drain. Stir in tomatoes and chiles. Set aside. Beat eggs and add flour, baking powder, salt, garlic, corn, sour cream, and cottage cheese. Mix well. Add rest of cheeses. Stir in sausage mixture. Pour into greased 9-by-13 pan. Bake at 350 degrees for 60–75 minutes until puffed and golden.

A Life That Says Welcome

This mouth-watering muffin recipe was featured in *Southern Living* magazine.

Mango-Macadamia Muffins

1 large egg
½ cup sour cream
½ cup milk
1 teaspoon vanilla
4 tablespoons butter, melted and cooled
1½ cups diced ripe mango
2 cups flour
½ cup sugar
1 tablespoon baking powder
¼ teaspoon baking soda
¼ teaspoon salt

Topping:

⅓ cup chopped unsalted macadamia nuts
¼ cup flour
¼ cup light brown sugar
¼ teaspoon cinnamon
2 tablespoons softened butter

For topping, combine all topping ingredients in a small bowl. Mash until combined. Chill until needed.

Preheat oven to 400 degrees. In a large bowl whisk together egg, sour cream, milk, vanilla, and melted butter. Fold in mango. In another bowl, stir together dry ingredients. Add wet ingredients. Fold together just to moisten. Batter will be lumpy. Quickly fill greased muffin tins with batter to the tops. Crumble topping over the tops. Bake 25–30 minutes until a toothpick inserted comes out with just a few crumbs clinging to it. Cool 5–10 minutes. Remove carefully from pans. Serve warm or at room temperature. Makes 12 muffins.

Finally, a decadent, delicious finger dessert unlike anything you've ever tasted!

Mocha Brownies

¾ cup unsalted butter, cut into pieces

4 ounces unsweetened chocolate, broken into
 pieces

2 tablespoons instant espresso powder or
 instant coffee

1 tablespoon boiling water

2 cups sugar

4 eggs

1 teaspoon vanilla extract

1 cup all-purpose flour

½ teaspoon baking powder

½ teaspoon salt

confectioner's sugar for dusting

Preheat oven to 350 degrees. Butter a 9-by-13 pan. In a bowl set over, but not touching, barely simmering water in a pan, combine the butter and chocolate. Stir with a wooden spoon until melted.

In a small bowl, dissolve the coffee powder in the boiling water. Add to the cooled chocolate. Then add the granulated sugar, eggs, and vanilla. Stir well. In another bowl, combine the flour, baking powder, and salt. Fold in the chocolate mixture until just incorporated. Pour the batter into the prepared pan. Bake until a wooden skewer inserted into the center comes out slightly fudgy, 25–30 minutes. Set the pan on a rack to cool. Cut into squares and dust with confectioner's sugar. Serve at room temperature. Store in a covered container (if they last that long!).

How to Host a Mug and Muffin

My friend Carmen and I decided we'd try holding a women's night out for our friends during the 1999 Christmas season. We sent out invitations, baked some muffins, put on the coffeepot, and waited. Nineteen ladies came to the first Mug and Muffin Moms' Night Out. We'd planned to do it twice a year. Instead, it turned into a monthly affair with over ninety moms on the mailing list, representing ten different churches and many who don't attend church. This ministry became so large that my church finally took it under their umbrella, and it is still going strong today.

If you'd like to start a similar ministry, whether large or small, here is how:

➷ Come up with an invitation list. Will you invite women from church, your workplace, your neighborhood, your children's school, or all of the above?

➷ On the invitations, tell the gals that hot drinks and muffins will be provided. All they need to bring is a mug (and perhaps $2.00 if you'd like help in covering the cost of the goodies, door prizes, and a speaker if you have one).

➷ Provide an assortment of homemade muffins and hot (or cold) drinks. Pass a basket around for ladies to place their name in a door prize drawing.

➷ Book a speaker or plan a theme. Many speakers are available on a variety of topics ranging from lighthearted to serious. We've had women speak on household organization, raising responsible kids, prayer, freezer cooking, summertime survival with kids, and marriage. If you'd rather hold a theme night, make it a brainstorming time such as "Everyone bring your best holiday de-stressing or cooking ideas" or "Bring your best home organization tips and storage ideas."

Practice Makes Perfect   215

❧ Purchase door prizes that go with the theme. If speaking on marriage, give away a dinner for two, some romantic candles, or a book on marriage. If the topic is quick cooking ideas, give away some kitchen utensils or a colander filled with everything needed for a pasta night—spaghetti noodles, pasta sauce, parmesan cheese, a loaf of French bread, etc.

❧ If appropriate, at the beginning of the meeting, break into groups of four or five. Share prayer requests and then have just one or two women from each group pray before returning to the large group.

❧ Rotate houses each time you meet so no one feels overburdened. Solicit muffin makers each time for the next meeting.

❧ Use the time between meetings to keep up with one another. Drop one of the gals a note or give someone a call to invite them to coffee. Use this ministry to forge friendships.

Hospitality Hall of Fame

While writing this book, I put the call out to women I've met during my speaking travels asking them to tell me about someone they knew whose life says "Welcome." Join me in meeting some of these dear women as we learn from their examples.

Holly Schurter

I was a bit apprehensive. I had to go to a meeting with several women I did not know, I had trouble finding the home where we were meeting, and I was the first to arrive. But my anxiety didn't last long because we were meeting in Holly's home.

Holly welcomed me into her home that day with a heartfelt smile and the smell of freshly baked cookies. I'd only known her for a few minutes, but she made me feel like I was a favorite friend.

I know our heavenly Father put Holly in my life for a purpose. I always look forward to connecting with her, whether in person or through email. She listens intently no matter what is going on around us, offers wise counsel, and always has encouragement to share. And oh, the comfort food!

But it's not just her cooking that provides comfort. Being a mom struggling to raise just two children, I'm comforted by Holly's ability to raise eight and still have a sense of humor. I'm comforted by her grace—a defining grace that can come only from a relationship with Christ.

In a recent sermon, our pastor shared a quote that made me immediately think of Holly: "You cannot offer hospitality to others unless you are completely at home with yourself." I'm so blessed to know her.

Contributed by Jennifer Gibson

Sue Kreiner

My friend Sue is a delightful inspiration because she takes on such huge tasks and does them so cheerfully. She is so generous, organized, and full of energy. She is not afraid to do the work it takes to make something special for someone.

Once she put on a "new moms' pampering day." She had a long row of several tables spread with linens and adorned with china out in her yard. She made them a perfect gourmet meal while they spent the day at different stations in her large home getting their nails done, their hair cut, beauty makeovers, and the like while some of us did childcare for their children and babies. When the meal was prepared, everyone went out to the row of tables and was served a leisurely long lunch in good company to complete their time together. Sue has eleven children of her own, homeschools them, does catering for large events, delivers babies, and looks like a teenager! And all with a smile and peaceful demeanor! She is the picture of hospitality.

Contributed by Piper Fountain

Grandma Sweetie and Her Pancakes

When my husband and I got married, my maternal grandparents sold us an acre of their land on the small farm that they owned. We built the house that we have raised our children in right next door. We never realized what a special blessing this would be to us.

Ashley and Drew were very small when they began their routine visits to Grandma and Grandpa Sweetie's. My grandparents inherited that name from their great-grandchildren because Grandma always called the kids "Sweetie," and so they called her Grandma Sweetie. The kids would go next door for many reasons, and they were always welcome. They shared endless bowls of ice cream or some homemade chocolate chip cookies together. They would pick flowers from the garden or just sit on the porch and talk. One of the favorite things to go to Grandma Sweetie's house for was "pancake dinner."

Once a week Grandma made Grandpa pancakes for dinner. It was a ritual between the two of them, something they always did and both enjoyed. When our children were around the ages of six and eight, they just happened to be around one of the evenings when Grandma made her pancakes for dinner and were invited to stay. When they came back home they couldn't stop talking about how delicious Grandma's pancakes were. Soon a pattern began to develop.

I noticed that the kids kept track of the days of the week and were very attentive to any mention of pancakes for dinner when

                    A Life That Says Welcome

they were around my grandparents. Grandma began to make sure she made a subtle announcement on the day she was making pancakes for dinner. I knew secretly she was hoping that those two little faces would be peering over her door window just about dinnertime.

Eventually, it became a tradition. Each week, on pancake night, four plates were set at the table instead of two. The kids would stop playing with friends to make sure they made it to Grandma's on time. They didn't want to do any extracurricular activities on the evenings pancakes were served for dinner. It was amazing to see the dedication and joy that was shared between the two generations over pancakes for dinner.

When our children were nine and eleven, Grandpa passed away, and Grandma followed six months later. Pancake dinners ended and were left to remain in the special place in the hearts of my children where the memories of their great-grandparents will live on forever. Some people have favorite recipes that are rich and elaborate. My children's favorite recipe is a pancake, made by the loving hands of a special Grandma Sweetie, that no one before or since has ever made as good as she did.

Contributed by Cindy Garrison

Patsy Conley

I have a close friend who is the mother of seven children. She doesn't care that much about how her house looks, but she always seems glad to see you, is always ready to invite you in, and acts like she has all the time in the world to just sit and talk.

She has the gift of being able to multitask. One year our daughter wanted to be Mother Teresa for Halloween and All Saints' Day. I called Patsy to see if she had a long white skirt in her costume box. She asked me why. When I told her, she said, "Go buy a twin flat sheet and some blue trim ribbon. Bring them

---

over and I'll make her Mother Teresa in an hour." I zoomed to the store and over to Patsy's. She sat down at her serger and sewing machines and whipped up a Mother Teresa costume within an hour while she was nursing a baby and instructing her other children on how to pack for a week-long trip they were leaving for in two hours! I will never forget that!

This is Patsy, as a young neighbor testified at a neighborhood party once. The young girl said, "The Conleys are moving. We will never again see Mrs. Conley standing at her stove cooking, smiling, nursing a baby, and teaching math to someone, all at the same time." No doubt this sister in the Lord has touched many lives with one word: *welcome*!

Contributed by Mary Jo Thayer

Sheila Shute

My mother has a way of making people feel welcome in her home. When she knows company is coming, she always has food made ahead, the house is neat and tidy, and she searches discount stores to add seasonal or themed plates, napkins, or centerpieces. She definitely works hard in advance to do all of the preparation work to make a wonderful atmosphere for her guests. She has begun a tradition with my children of "pillow treats." Whenever we come for an overnight visit, she puts "pillow treats" where each of the boys will be sleeping. These are little things that she has picked up at the dollar store—anything from their favorite candy bar to a Hot Wheels car or a pack of sports cards. They absolutely *love* it! They run in her door, give her a hug and kiss, and then run straight for their sleeping spots to uncover their treats! This tradition is so fun to watch. It shows my boys that she cares, she knows what they like, and she is glad they are there. My boys have now started making pillow treats for Grammy when she comes to stay at our house. They make her homemade cards and

A Life That Says Welcome

notes, and they want to go shopping for Grammy's pillow treat items before she comes!

Contributed by Lesa Bruns

JoAnne Bierma

Imagine a new city, a new church, a new women's small group, and a first-time mom with her four-month-old infant in her arms walking hesitantly into the room. The women, in all stages of life, knew one another well and had already formed a tight-knit circle without an empty seat among them.

Then JoAnne looked up, motioned the young mom to sit by her, brought a chair into the circle, cooed over the baby, and welcomed me into her heart for the next seventeen years.

JoAnne lives a life of welcome by design. She leaves her time open to the moment, without busy family schedules, so she can meet the needs of family and friends whenever and wherever they need her.

As I nursed three babies in her home over the years, she always placed me in her best comfy chair, brought a big glass of cool water, found pillows to support the baby, placed my feet up on a nursing stool, and played soft music to relax everyone.

When I had toddlers and preschoolers in tow, she set up toys in a room close by just for them, invited them into her vegetable garden to pick their own snack, and enjoyed their company and conversation.

Once all my children were in school, she sent home gently used toys or clothing for them from her own children. Often she attached a note or shared a memory about how her older children had enjoyed that toy or the adventures they'd had while wearing each piece of clothing.

When she welcomes me into her home today, she sets a simple but beautiful place setting. She cooks a nutritious meal to feed

---

Practice Makes Perfect

my body "so you can meet the needs of your family later today." Then she nourishes my soul with laughter, perspective, wisdom, and prayer by giving me her complete attention.

JoAnne still mothers a younger mother, who is a season behind her, and challenges me to do the same for another young mom who may walk into my own tight-knit circle someday.

Contributed by Mary Steinke

In Memory of Reginald and Velma Beaufore

When I married into my husband's family, I began to witness firsthand a family that lived a life of unselfish hospitality. Their doors were forever open, as well as their hearts. There was always room for one more on the couch or at the supper table. At the holidays, I saw their love for others really come alive. When a holiday was approaching, they would ask, "Well, who is coming for Christmas this year?" Now, they didn't just mean what relatives would grace us with their presence. They wanted to know what outsiders would be intentionally grafted into their family structure that year.

The Beaufores felt that the Christmas season was a perfect excuse to make someone's life better, and they did it as often as they could. They were well known for taking in orphans from the local orphanage for several days over Christmas. They made them a part of their family. They showered them with love and any little gifts they could afford. Once they kept a little girl named Cheryl for several days. She told them she wanted to live with them so badly. So they adopted her! She was in great need of medical attention in many areas, and they sought it out for her just as if she were their very own.

Though they are gone, I still remember the tangible ways they showed love to others even with sometimes limited resources.

A Life That Says Welcome

The world would be a better place with more giving and caring people like them.

Contributed by Jerry Beaufore

Winnie Gill

I met my husband in Bible college in North Carolina. He was from Michigan and I was from Virginia. During our college years, his grandma decided to bless me with a home-cooked Thanksgiving meal sent all the way from Michigan since my family had eaten Thanksgiving dinner at a restaurant that year. My husband-to-be returned from the holiday with Grandma's delicious meal in coolers, and he then warmed it up in a dormitory microwave just for me. I remember feeling so honored and blessed by Grandma's hospitable meal on wheels!

We were married just after my husband's college graduation, and then we moved to Michigan. I began my life as a new bride, but I still missed my family so much. My grandma-in-love sought out ways to bless me and help me in this new stage of life. She provided countless hours of babysitting, many delicious meals to celebrate birthdays and holidays, and wonderful conversations over tea and cookies.

Grandma is also a faithful prayer warrior. She is quick to encourage us to "pray about it, honey," and also quick to remind us of the awesome power of prayer. She enriches the lives of all whom she touches. Recently widowed, she is living out such a beautiful walk with the Lord and leaving such a godly legacy for her great-grandchildren, who call her "Grams." She is a beautiful example of a woman of hospitality. I think of Grandma when I read Philippians 2:3–4: "Do nothing out of selfish ambition or vain conceit, but in humility consider others better than yourselves. Each of you should look not only to your own interests, but also

---

to the interests of others." I am richly blessed to have Winnie Gill as my grandma-in-love.

Contributed by Julie Gill

Year-Round Get-Togethers

As the seasons change, so can your reasons for hosting company. Learn to celebrate anything. Have another family over for cherry pie on Presidents' Day or Irish stew on Saint Patrick's Day. Any excuse is good enough for a get-together! Have fun with some of these creative get-together ideas contributed by my friend Teena Sands.

Hobo Dinner

Eat off tin pie plates and drink from glass jars. Use a bandana for a napkin. Serve hamburger patties, loaded baked potatoes with all the fixings, and pieces of fruit for dessert.

70s Party

Ask guests to come dressed in bell-bottoms, tie-dye, and leisure suits. Have lava lamps around and play 70s music like Abba. Dinner is fondue with meat and fruit and chocolate. Hang beads in the doorway. Play charades.

Camping Dinner

Set up a tent in the backyard for the kids to play in. Serve hot dogs off the grill, baked beans, and s'mores. Make a bonfire if you are able. Sing campfire songs and tell stories or give testimonies of how God is at work in the lives of the attendees.

Mystery Dinner

Invite a couple over for dinner and ask them to invite a "mystery couple" to join you, preferably someone you don't know very well. You never know who's coming to dinner!

Back-to-School Party

Before school starts up in the fall, we serve a special lunch to the moms we know. Every year I make a school-themed cake. Last year was an apple. This year will be a ruler. We have a prayer time for the kids as they go back to school, whether homeschool or traditional. Decorate the table with new school supplies. Play Back-to-School Bingo, making game cards using school terms like recess, gymnasium, glue stick, and lunch box. Award small prizes like stickers. Borrow school trays from a local school and drink milk from small cartons, or serve the kids lunch in a lunch box.

Lesa Bruns offers this back-to-school gathering idea: "We live in a neighborhood with lots of families with school-aged children. There are twenty-one children at our bus stop! One tradition we have begun is to have a back-to-school cul-de-sac party for our bus stop families the weekend before the kids go back to school. We pull the grill into the end of the cul-de-sac and throw on some burgers and hot dogs. Every family brings a dish to share and a cooler with drinks. One mom agrees to bring paper plates, napkins, and plastic silverware. The kids play, and everyone shares highlights from their summer. It is a great way to transition into the next season and catch up with neighbors!"

Soup's On!

Throw a soup party. I like to invite some friends over for lunch and serve three or four different soups. Usually I try a few new recipes and a few favorites. Add warm, homemade bread and a simple dessert like a fruit cobbler, and you have a satisfying lunch. This is great for the fall.

Bless at the Holidays

We had an Operation Christmas Child Party one year right before Thanksgiving. Everyone brought twelve of one item (soap, combs, play dough, crayons, candy, toy cars, etc.). I had some things purchased as well. Samaritan's Purse (www .samaritanspurse.org) sent me the boxes, which didn't have to be wrapped, and a video of their ministry. We started the party by watching the video as a group while some of the mothers laid out all the items on my dining room table. After the video, I talked to the kids about what we were going to be doing and how our shoe boxes would be showing Jesus to other children around the world. The children then took their shoe boxes and walked around the table choosing items to put in. We had some refreshments, made cards to go into the boxes, and then prayed for the ones who would be receiving them. One thing I loved about this party was that it was a giving party. No one went home with a treat bag.

My Hospitable Hubby

"Hey, Hon. Do we have enough food for two more?"

This is a familiar question coming over the walkie-talkie at our house. My husband calls from the workshop across the lane, generally just minutes before I call him and our two sons in for lunch or dinner. My answer is always, "Of course! Just give me fifteen minutes."

He knows I can make four boneless chicken breasts and three ears of corn look like a feast in minutes just by cutting everything

A Life That Says Welcome

in half and adding a couple of side dishes. He also knows I can't make our house look like the cover story for *Better Homes and Gardens* in the same few minutes.

The problem is, that's exactly what he expects.

One Thanksgiving he came into the kitchen looking incredulous and said, "I thought you said you had everything ready." I looked out the window—our family was walking up the driveway. I looked in the dining room. The table was set (and sparkling, I might add), the turkey was cooking, pots were boiling, drinks were ready.

"I do. What's missing?"

"There are dirty clothes in there." He pointed to the laundry room.

"Yes."

"The laundry should be done when we're having company."

I don't remember now whether I laughed out loud or just to myself. I am truly not embarrassed by laundry. We have tons of it, living on a farm, near a creek, with two boys, a dog, and a husband with a workshop. I do several loads of laundry every day. If someone enters through my back door into the laundry/mud room, that's what they're going to see—laundry and mud. Everyone has laundry.

My husband also believes the furniture should be moved every time I vacuum, the toilet *tanks* should be cleaned out regularly, and the garage should be as clean and neat as the rest of the house . . . *should be.*

So how do I make hospitality stress-free for both of us? It's not always easy. And I admit, it's not always stress-free. But people keep coming back, and my husband keeps inviting them, so we must be doing something right!

One of the best hints I ever took was to look into my house from the outside. Do it several different times—when it's dark out and the lights are on inside, when you think it looks "just fine," and when you know it's a mess. I found that my secret hiding place for papers and mail was in direct view from the kitchen door most guests use!

I really try to keep the surfaces—tables, countertops, even the floor—cleared off all the time. The island in our kitchen gets cluttered every day, but I know I can stack the stuff up and hide it in my roll-top desk in the office in just seconds. And I force myself to dedicate every Thursday morning to cleaning off that rolltop desk.

If I have the chance, I close the garage door. Even with the key-pad, my husband will walk around to the front door if that garage door is closed. Then he won't see that the laundry isn't done.

I always do the things I don't want anyone to *see* me do first. If they're coming for dinner, they can see me cook. But if they don't see me wipe up the bathroom, fill a grocery bag with stray toys, and maybe change into a clean shirt or brush my hair, they don't know it needed to be done.

After twenty years of marriage, the best thing I've learned to do is to give *him* jobs. I used to fret about what he expected, almost to the point of ruining the evening for myself. Now I can just whisper, "Honey, would you go check the bathroom and close the laundry room door?" He usually does a more thorough job than I would—and he actually *likes* that I thought about it and wanted something done about it!

It is very important to know your spouse's comfort level with household clutter when entertaining guests, whether the guests are expected or not. I think that in most households, the wife is pickier. In our house, it's the opposite. I'm more concerned with how my guests feel than what the house looks like. However, I also need to think about what my husband feels. We have a lot more fun when we're both happy!

Contributed by Lynda Rettick

A Life That Says Welcome

⤲ 11 ⤳

God's Bigger Picture

We stopped at the wayside rest area to get a little something to eat, refill our water bottles, and stretch our legs a bit. It was a long trip from our home in the center of Michigan to my Aunt Patty and Uncle Lee's place in beautiful northern Wisconsin. This particular wayside had an interesting gift shop stocked with many items found in nature. There were interesting snarled pieces of driftwood, colorful Native American artifacts, stunning copper bracelets and turquoise jewelry, and over a hundred varieties of seashells. Our three kids made their way down the aisles, studying the treasures.

At the end of an aisle sat a turnstile display sporting whimsical kitchen mugs, the personalized kind with a first name printed on the side. One of the boys spied it and alerted his siblings to this fun find. Soon all three kids were giving the rack the once-over. What were they looking for?

You guessed it: each one was looking for his or her own name. No matter if the name of a neighbor was there, or a cousin or friend. Each child longingly looked for their own personal string of letters in a row, the one that would spell out "me" to them.

Oh, we've all done the same thing in different ways. When we get our family reunion pictures, high school class yearbook, or church pictorial directory, something within us drives us to pick up those items and determine, "Where am *I* at in this?"

Dear ones, don't we do the same in so much of our lives? Whether it is the coming long weekend, the family vacation, or the afternoon shopping trip or outing, what we really want to know, whether we verbalize it or not, is "What's in it for me?" It is a fight against the flesh that wants to elevate self, to cater to our own wants, to whine "It's all about me."

Oh, how this concept plays out when we contemplate the prospect of offering hospitality to others or when we are suddenly thrown into a situation where being a hostess seems inevitable. An out-of-town friend passing through your town suddenly lands on your front stoop, Uncle Henry announces he's coming to stay for a week, or you receive a call from the missions committee chair requesting that you have a visiting missionary family over for supper after church next week. What is your initial response?

If you are like me, your very first thoughts aren't always the epitome of niceness. Far from it. My selfish little brain can create dozens of excuses in such a short time, it will make your head spin. The timing isn't right, or the family is too busy, or we have other plans that simply can't be changed. Now, granted, once in a while that may be true. But more often than not, the truth is, there just isn't anything in it for little ol' me!

We need to broaden our horizons, to check the big picture, to see the world as God sees it. We need to take off our self-magnifying monocle and instead replace it with God's 20/20 perspective. He sees the big picture. He knows why we have been chosen to be his hands and his feet to this dear individual or that family temporarily in our midst. If we were only more willing, we could see him work in wonderful ways, using us in the process. We could have a front row seat in the theater of his involvement in others' lives. Oh, I know the glimpses I have gotten of this spectacular show have been more exciting than anything Hollywood could dream up! And I'm ashamed of the times I have let my own selfish ways set the agenda and cancel out the part God had written for me to play.

The older I get, the more convinced I become of this: we will experience firsthand the workings of God in direct proportion to our willingness to play the precise part he has chosen for us. So often we want to be the star of the show. But may I suggest to you that taking on a supporting role, however small and seemingly insignificant, is often where God would rather have us be. I am thankful for the times he has been able to use me and my family in spite of ourselves to encourage a weary traveler along life's journey. Sometimes we don't even realize the part we played until years later.

I have often run into a former cheerleader I coached, a now-grown youth group member, or an old neighbor, and they have expressed to me how much they were blessed by an action, a touch, a homemade goodie, or a welcoming visit in our not-too-distant past. Sometimes I am nearly reduced to tears knowing that at the time I was fighting with God, repeatedly ignoring his promptings, and then finally acting on his urgings just to get him off my back, for crying out loud! Oh, how much easier life would be if we cooperated with our Creator!

The Hand-Heart Connection

So now we are nearing the homestretch. I hope this book has presented you with some tools to assist you in your quest to become a hospitable hostess and a welcoming woman. Now take your place in the picture God is directing in your life at this moment. But please remember, the most important tool you will need is a willing heart. With a heart that says, "Here I am, Lord. Use me," there is no limit to the amount of good God can do and the infinite measure of blessing that will be bounced back to you in return.

But before I leave you, let me ask you two questions: What is in your heart? And what is in your hand?

What is in your heart? What are you passionate about? What issues of the Christian life spark your interest? Do you have a particular talent or hobby that you enjoy teaching others how to do? Can you sew? (Please come to my house. My children's AWANA badges are attached with hot glue!) Do you possess an ever-green thumb and a garden that is the envy of all on your block? Do you have a desire to teach new moms the basics of childcare or beginning brides what it means to be a godly wife? Are you a whiz at the computer? Does your passion for God's Word make you perfect to disciple a brand-new believer? Think about it for a moment: *what is in your heart?*

Now look down. What is in your hand?

What are you already doing in this stage of your life that God could take and broaden in order to bless others? I ask you again: what is in your hand?

Is it a trowel or hoe? If you grow beautiful flowers that bring joy to you and to passersby, don't leave them all in the ground. Snip a bouquet and deliver it to a widow, some shut-ins, or a suddenly single mom. Take your hospitality *and* your flowers on the road. Are the tomatoes ready and ripe on the vine? I think I can hear the whirl of the blender as you turn them into freshly made Mexican salsa. Someone you know would love to be invited over to share a batch, dipping deep into it with some crisp corn tortilla chips while sharing your company.

Look down. What is in your hand?

Is it your well-worn copper teakettle or new-fangled coffeepot? You can make enough for two, you know. Put the pot on. Pick up the phone. Invite. Invest.

At your fingertips is there a computer keyboard? I'll bet you have a neighbor who is at a loss for how to use one. Give her a free lesson and a tall glass of lemonade as well.

Or is it a pen and piece of pretty stationery? Could you take the time, say once a week or so, and set aside a few moments to resurrect the nearly forgotten art of handwriting a note to a stranger or friend? Bless others with your words and with God's. Tell them he is crazy about them and that you love them too. Tell them not to give up, to persist and pursue. Speak to their spirit with that pen in your hand.

What else do you hold? Is it a mop or a broom? Could you use it to venture to the home of a first-time mother? Offer your services to her. For these first few tiring weeks of life, clean her place once every week while she and the new baby nap. She will so appreciate it, believe me. There is no tired like newborn baby tired!

Look down. What do you see? Is your Bible open on your lap? Ask God to lead you this year to someone who needs to learn how to study his precepts for themselves.

Is within your tight grip a spatula or wooden spoon? Could you bake a batch or cook a dish that would nourish both stomach and soul? Could you double your planned portion and set a few extra places at tonight's table? You must know someone who could use a hot meal and would be blessed by sharing it with others.

But what if what you hold in your hand ties you down? Is it a sleeping baby or wriggly child? Is it something you think hinders you from this call because it occupies your time and expends your energy?

That's fine. God sees and understands. And he has placed you in just such a place for a reason. It doesn't mean we put our lives on hold and assume that we are exempt from offering welcome. Perhaps we are to be offering welcome first to that little one or to the very person we feel is holding us back from reaching out. I know where you are. I was in just such a position for what seemed like many years but in retrospect was really a short time in my life. And it was the exact place where God began to deal with my attitude and subsequent actions. It was there I learned to bloom where I was planted and quit trying to live someone else's life. It was there that I learned what sweet author Elisabeth Elliot once wrote: "The difference is Christ in me. Not me in a different set of circumstances."

I've seen others live this truth out loud—like my close friend Marcia Stump. She has struggled with many sicknesses and diseases in her own life, not to mention caring for a son who was hospitalized with a life-threatening infection, another who survived a serious car crash, a husband who was diagnosed recently with leukemia, and a best friend who died in her presence after a two-year-long battle with breast cancer.

Marcia took our friend Julie to many doctor's appointments and chemotherapy treatments during her courageous fight with cancer. Due to her own family illnesses, Marcia has also spent countless hours in hospital waiting rooms and medical holding tanks surrounded by other patients, family members, doctors, and staff. She has become well acquainted with waiting, sorrow, sickness, and grief.

But do you know what amazes me about Marcia? This woman doesn't react like I fear I would react. She doesn't plead, "Lord, get me out of here!" Instead she quietly asks, "Lord, why have you brought me here?" She looks beyond her own pain and sorrow to make sure she doesn't miss a God-given opportunity for blessing or a seemingly chance meeting with someone he wants her to cheer. I wonder just how many precious souls my friend Marcia has touched with welcome and care in the midst of her not-so-lovely circumstances. You too can be hospitable wherever you are!

So my prayer for you is that you will embrace your lot in life. Don't spend your days wishing you were someone else, that you owned their fine things or lived in their fancy home, or that you were living their apparently wonderful life. Don't miss the miracles that are waiting to unfold right before your very eyes as you eagerly say, "Here I am, Lord. Use me." He has a story to write, and you are an integral part of it, no matter how large or small the role.

The stage is set. Take your place. Hit your mark. Position your hands. Open your heart.

Here comes someone now . . .

Smile and say, "Welcome!"

Karen Ehman is a graduate of Spring Arbor University with a B.A. in social science. She has been married for twenty years to Todd and is the homeschooling mother of three children. She is the former editor of *A Mother's Mission Newsletter* and a free-lance writer and contributor to the *Proverbs 31 Newsletter* and the *Hearts at Home* magazine, a ministry for which she also teaches workshops and is the director of drama. A sought-after speaker for women's events, conferences, and retreats, she is also the creator of the *Hearts at Home Mom's Planner*, an organizational tool designed specifically for the purpose of helping mothers organize their personal, family, and devotional life. She has been a guest on national television and radio programs including *At Home Live, Engaging Women, The Harvest Show, Moody Midday Connection*, and Dr. James Dobson's *Focus on the Family*. She recently began her own weekly radio spot entitled *The Keep It Simple Woman* heard on 91.5 WCIC FM in central Illinois. Before motherhood, Karen was a teacher and cheerleading coach. Though hopelessly craft challenged, she enjoys baking and cooking and has won several blue ribbon rosettes at various county fairs for her cookies, cakes, pies, and breads. This is her third book.

If you would like more information on having Karen speak to your group or at your womens' event, email her at KarenEhman@FamilyClassroom.net for details and a list of her speaking topics.

Your go-to guide to making
holidays, birthdays, special events, and even the

everyday special.

"*Everyday Confetti* is going to make me look like Superwoman—
if there ever were such a thing!"

—CANDACE CAMERON BURE, actress; coauthor of the *New York Times*
bestseller *Reshaping It All*